Jeffery Carr

Murphy's Law & Military Maxims

novum pro

All rights of distribution, including via film, radio, and television, photomechanical reproduction, audio storage media, electronic data storage media, and the reprinting of portions of text, are reserved.

© 2019 novum publishing

ISBN 978-1-64268-095-9
Editing: Karen Simmering
Cover photo:
Okanakdeniz | Dreamstime.com
Cover design, layout & typesetting: novum publishing
Internal illustrations:
see bibliography p.231

www.novumpublishing.com

By LTC Jeff Carr (Ret.)

This book is dedicated to my mentors SGM James M. Carr, SGM Gary A. Marshman & CSM Jesse A. Ramil, as well as to all of the warriors who have suffered from the slings and arrows of Murphy's wrath. Also, special thanks to my friend and colleague, COL Bruce Irwin for assisting in the development of this book.

INTRODUCTION

While serving as a tactics instructor at the U.S. Army Command & General Staff College, I was mindful of the adage that the *"mind can only absorb what the ass can endure."* As such, in the effort to minimize my students suffering from long-winded lectures I often relied upon using the humorous, simple illustrations contained in this book to reinforce their understanding of the proven maxims of the great military leaders such as Sun Tzu, Caesar and Napoleon, as well as the pitfalls associated with poor planning and execution.

For those who are academically inclined, I have also provided a list of suggested books that will equip them with greater insight as to how to minimize their exposure in becoming a victim of that pesky character known as Murphy.

MAXIM #1

YOU ARE NOT SUPERMAN

*Painting Title: Napoleon on Campaign –
The Retreat from Moscow by Ernest Meissonier (1815–1891)*

The Russian victory over the French army in 1812 marked a huge blow to Napoleon's ambitions of European dominance and similarly revealed that he was not, in fact, invincible, thus ending his reputation as a military genius. Of the initial 690,000 men of the *Grande Armée* that assembled on June 24, 1812 to cross the river Neman to head toward Moscow, only 40,000 frost-bitten and starved soldiers managed to return to France.

Painting Title: The Battle of Lützen by Carl Wahlbom (1810–1858)

In 1627, near Dirschau in Prussia, King Gustavus II Adolphus was shot in the upper shoulder by a Polish soldier. When his doctors proved unsuccessful in removing the bullet, he from that point thereafter, elected to never again don his cuirass, claiming that the weight of it only served to exacerbate his injury. On November 16, 1632, he was reported to have entered the Battle of Lützen without wearing any armor, proclaiming, "The Lord God is my armor" and was later mortally wounded.

MAXIM #1

YOU ARE NOT SUPERMAN

General Sedgwick at the Battle of Gettysburg

Major General John Sedgwick – Civil War Union VI Corps Commander – was mortally wounded while directing artillery placements at the Battle of the Wilderness, Spotsylvania on May 9, 1864. After witnessing both his staff officers and artillerymen seeking cover from sporadic Confederate sniper fire from approximately 1,000 yards away, he openly paraded on the battlefield and reportedly exclaimed, "What? Men dodging this way for single bullets? What will you do when they open fire on the whole line? I am ashamed of you. Nonsense, they couldn't hit an elephant from this distance!" Minutes later, he was struck by a bullet below his left eye. General Sedgwick was the highest-ranking Union officer killed during the Civil War.

MAXIM #1
YOU ARE NOT SUPERMAN

Statue of Achilles Dying in the Gardens of the Achilleion

In Greek mythology, Achilles (the son of the sea-nymph Thetis and the mortal Peleus, king of the Myrmidons in Thessaly) was arguably the greatest hero of the Trojan War (most scholars date the war to the 12th or 13th century BC) and the central character of Homer's epic poem Iliad. While a child, Achilles' mother sought to make her son immortal by dipping him into the river Styx, by which his whole body became invulnerable, except that part of his heel by which she held him, whence came the proverbial "heel of Achilles." After the death of his friend Patrocles, Achilles avenged his death by killing Hector, the Trojan champion, and forever sealed his legacy as one of history's greatest warriors. However, despite Achilles' prowess on the battlefield, it was ultimately his amorous nature that led to his tragic demise. After killing Prince Troilus, the son of King Priam, in a duel occurring at the sanctuary of Apollo, he was lured by the vengeful but beautiful Trojan Princess Polyxena (Troilus' sister) to Troy, where her other brother, Paris (history's great lover) ambushed him and shot a fatal arrow that pierced his exposed heel.

MAXIM #1

YOU ARE NOT SUPERMAN

Statue of Marshal Turenne

Henri de La Tour d'Auvergne –The Vicomte de Turenne was one of France's greatest marshals who served during the reign of Louis XIV. He began his military career in the Thirty Years War (from 1625) and subsequently commanded the royal armies in the civil war of the Fronde (1648–53) in the French invasion of the Spanish Netherlands (1667), and in the third Dutch War (beginning in 1672). He possessed a strategic grasp of the principles of fire and maneuver and typically positioned himself where he could best influence the battle. While examining a position at the battle of Salzbach on 27 July, 1675, Turenne was killed by a cannon shot and upon being hit exclaimed, "I did not mean to be killed today." He was buried with the kings of France at Saint-Denis but later, Napoleon, who deemed him one of history's greatest military leaders, had his remains transferred to the Invalides in Paris.

MAXIM #1

YOU ARE NOT SUPERMAN

David Slays Goliath from Victorian Book "The Child's Bible," 1883

1 Samuel 17 – New International Version (NIV)
David and Goliath

Now the Philistines gathered their forces for war and assembled at Sokoh in Judah. They pitched camp at Ephes Dammim, between Sokoh and Azekah. Saul and the Israelites assembled and camped in the Valley of Elah and drew up their battle line to meet the Philistines. The Philistines occupied one hill and the Israelites another, with the valley between them. A champion named Goliath, who was from Gath, came out of the Philistine camp. His height was six cubits and a span (roughly 9'9"). He had a bronze helmet and wore a coat of scale armor of bronze weighing five thousand shekels (125 lbs. or 58 kilograms). On his legs he wore bronze greaves and he slung a bronze javelin on his back. His spear shaft was like a weaver's rod, and its iron point weighed six hundred shekels (15 lbs or 6.9 kilograms) His shield bearer went ahead of him.

    Goliath stood and shouted to the ranks of Israel, "Why do you come out and line up for battle? Am I not a Philistine, and are you not the servants of Saul? Choose a man and have him come down to me. If he is able to fight and kill me, we will become your subjects; but if I overcome him and kill him, you will become our subjects and serve us." Then the Philistine said, "This day I defy the armies of Israel! Give me a man and let us fight each other." On hearing the Philistine's words, Saul and all the Israelites were dismayed and terrified.

    For forty days the Philistine came forward every morning and evening and took his stand and issued his insults. Ultimately, David, a young shepherd boy dressed in a simple tunic and equipped with his shepherd's staff, slingshot and a pouch full of stones responded to the challenge of the Philistine champion. As Goliath moved in to kill David, the boy reached into his bag and slung one of his stones at the giant's head. Finding a hole in the armor, the stone sank into his forehead and he had fallen face down to the ground. David then ran and stood over him. He took hold of the Philistine's sword and drew it from the sheath and cut off his head with the sword. When the Philistines saw that their hero was dead, they retreated with the Israelites pursing and killing them and eventually plundering their camp.

MAXIM #1

YOU ARE NOT SUPERMAN

Painting of Marshal Ney by Francois Gerard – (1770–1837)

Marshal of France, Michel Ney
January 10, 1769–December 7, 1815

Michel Ney was a French soldier and military commander during the Revolutionary Wars and the Napoleonic Wars. He was one of the original eighteen Marshals of France promoted by Napoleon. He was known as *Le Rougeaud* ("red faced" or "ruddy") by his men and later nicknamed *le Brave des Braves* ("the bravest of the brave") by Napoleon during the retreat from Moscow in 1812, when he commanded the rear guard and was reputed to have been the last Frenchman to leave Russian soil.

In 1815, when Paris fell, and the Bourbons reclaimed the throne, Ney pressured Napoleon to accept his first abdication and exile and was promoted and made a peer by the newly enthroned Louis XVIII. Later, upon hearing of Napoleon's escape from Elba, Ney organized a force to stop Napoleon's march on Paris, pledging to bring Napoleon back alive in an iron cage. Napoleon, aware of Ney's plan, sent him a letter which said, in part, "I shall receive you as after the Battle of the Moscow." Despite Ney's promise to the King to arrest Napoleon, he joined his beloved commander at Auxerre on March 18, 1815.

On June 15, 1815, Napoleon appointed Ney commander of the left wing of the Army of the North. On 16 June Napoleon's forces split up into two wings to fight two separate battles simultaneously. Ney attacked Wellington at Quatre Bras while Napoleon attacked Blücher's Prussians at Ligny.

Shortly thereafter, at Waterloo, Ney again commanded the left wing of the army and ordered a mass cavalry-charge against the Anglo-Allied line. Ney's cavalry overran the enemy cannons, but found the infantry formed in cavalry-proof square formations. Ney, without infantry or artillery support, failed to break the squares and his cavalry also failed to spike enemy cannon while they were under French control (during the cavalry attack, the crews of the cannon retreated into the squares for protection, and then re-manned their pieces as the horsemen receded). Ney was seen during one of the charges beating his sword against the side of British cannon in furious frustration. During the battle, in keeping with his audacious leadership style, he had five horses killed under him.

When Napoleon was ultimately defeated, dethroned, and exiled for the second time in the summer of 1815, Ney was arrested on August 3, 1815 and tried on December 4, 1815 for treason by the Chamber of Peers. On December 6, 1815 he was condemned and executed by a firing squad in Paris on December 7, 1815. When offered a blindfold, he summarily refused and requested that he be allowed the right to give the order to fire. His last words purportedly were "Soldiers, when I give the command to fire, fire straight at my heart. Wait for the order. It will be my last to you. I protest against my condemnation. I have fought a hundred battles for France, and not one against her ... Soldiers, Fire!"

MAXIM #1

YOU ARE NOT SUPERMAN

"The Mighty King of Chivalry Richard the Lionheart"
painted by Fortunino Matania – (1881–1961)

Richard I, king of England from 1189 to 1199, was the personification of the "Warrior King." His fierceness in battle during the Third Crusade won him the title of Lionheart and even his most formidable enemy, Saladin, respected Richard and feared his army. Saladin's own emirs were terrified of the warrior they called Malek Rik. For decades following Richard's crusade, Muslim mothers called upon his name to frighten their children into behaving.

Despite his legendary heart of a lion in battle and his seeming invincibility, he ultimately met his untimely death while suppressing a revolt by Viscount Aimar V of Limoges. More specifically, after devastating the viscount's land with fire and sword, he besieged a small and virtually unarmed castle of Chalus-Chabrol because a local peasant had claimed to uncover a treasure trove of Roman gold which Richard now claimed as Aimar's feudal overlord.

In the early evening of March 25, 1199, Richard was walking around the castle perimeter without his chainmail, investigating the progress of sappers on the castle walls. Although arrows were occasionally shot from the castle walls, Richard paid little attention except to one defender in particular, who was standing on the castle walls with a crossbow in one hand and the other clutching a frying pan as a shield to deflect incoming missiles. While applauding this man for both his temerity and persistence, he was ultimately struck in the left shoulder near the neck by another crossbowman. He then retreated to the privacy of his tent in order to extract the arrow himself but failed to do so. His surgeon, referred to by one of his chroniclers as a "butcher," carelessly removed it but managed to mangle his arm in the process and the wound eventually became gangrenous.

After the castle was taken, Richard asked to have the crossbowman that inflicted the soon fatal blow brought before him. To his astonishment, his enemy happened to be merely a boy who honorably sought revenge for Richard's troops killing his father and two brothers and the lad then indicated that he was prepared to be executed. Richard, as his last act of mercy and abiding respect for the boy's moral and physical courage, forgave him of the crime and famously rejoined, "Live on, and by my bounty behold the light of day," before ordering him to be freed and sent away with 100 shillings. Richard then set his affairs in order, bequeathing all his territory to his brother John and his jewels to his nephew Otto and then died on April 6, 1199.

Because of the nature of Richard's death, he was later referred to as 'the Lion (that) by the Ant was slain.' According to one chronicler, Richard's last act of chivalry proved fruitless; in an orgy of medieval brutality, the infamous mercenary captain Mercadier had the crossbowman flayed alive and hanged as soon as Richard died.

MAXIM #1

YOU ARE NOT SUPERMAN

Michael Wittman – Known as the "Black Baron" in reference to the "Red Baron" World War I Fighter Ace – Manfred von Richthofen.

Michael Wittman (April 22, 1914–August 8, 1944) was a German *Waffen-SS* tank commander during the Second World War and rose to the rank of SS-*Hauptsturmführer* (Captain). He was awarded the Knight's Cross with Swords and Oak Leaves of the Iron Cross.

He was credited with the destruction of 138 tanks and 132 anti-tank guns, along with an unknown number of other armored vehicles, making him one of Germany's top scoring panzer aces.

Wittman, a serious practitioner of *Blitzkrieg* (Lighting War) commented the following after observing the Allied landing at D-Day in June 1944, "… the decision was a very, very difficult one. Never before had I been so impressed by the strength of the enemy as I was by those tanks rolling by; but I knew it absolutely had to be and I decided to strike out into the enemy."

Accordingly, on June 13, 1944, during the Battle of Villers-Bocage, Wittman, while in command of a single *Panzerkampfwagen VI Tiger*, ambushed elements of the British 7th Armored Division and destroyed 14 tanks, 15 personnel carriers and 2 anti-tank guns within the space of 15 minutes.

Wittmann was killed on August 8,1944 while taking part in a counterattack ordered by Colonel Kurt Meyer of the 12th SS Panzer Division to retake tactically important high ground near the town of Saint-Aignan-de-Cramesnil. The town and surrounding high ground had been captured a few hours earlier by Anglo-Canadian forces during Operation Totalize. Wittmann had decided to participate in the attack as he believed the company commander who was supposed to lead the attack was too inexperienced.

A group of seven Tiger tanks from the Heavy SS-Panzer Battalion 101, supported by several other tanks, was ambushed by tanks from A Squadron, 1st Northamptonshire Yeomanry, A Squadron, the Sherbrooke Fusilier Regiment, and B Squadron, the 144 Royal Armoured Corps.

The killing shots originated from a Sherman Firefly of '3 Troop,' A Squadron, 1st Northamptonshire which was positioned in a wood called Delle de la Roque on the advancing Tigers' right flank. It appears the shells penetrated the upper hull of Wittman's tank and ignited the Tiger's own ammunition, thereby causing a fire which engulfed the tank and then blew off the turret. Upon hearing of his untimely death, *SS-Obergruppenfuhrer* Josef "Sepp" Dietrich best summarized his accomplishments as a gallant, audacious warrior by stating, "He was a fighter in every way, he lived and breathed action."

MAXIM

1 LESSON LEARNED

WWII German Military Cemetery in Vazec, Slovakia

"The paths of glory lead but to the grave." – Gray's Elegy in a Country Churchyard

The Grim Reaper does not discriminate when claiming his victims, no matter how bold and courageous. Humility coupled with judicious prudence may be the critical factor in surviving the horrors of combat and ultimately securing your military objective.

MAXIM #2
IF IT APPEARS STUPID BUT WORKS, IT ISN'T STUPID

Photo of Fu-Go Incendiary Balloon Bomb

Reacting to General Jimmy Doolittle's B-25 bomber raid over Japan in the spring of 1942, the Japanese launched 9,000 "Fusen bakudan" fire balloons (a hydrogen balloon varying from 26 lb incendiary to a 33 lb antipersonnel bomb) across the Pacific Ocean, of which 300 were found or observed in the United States. In fact, on March 10, 1945, one of these balloons had descended near the Manhattan Project's production site at Hanford, Washington and landed on a power line that fed electricity to the building containing the reactor producing plutonium for the Nagasaki bomb, and shut the reactor down. Although largely ineffectual, this weapon still managed to kill six Americans and caused minor property damage both in the United States and Canada.

MAXIM #2

IF IT APPEARS STUPID BUT WORKS, IT ISN'T STUPID

Photo of Russian Attack Dog under Tank

During World War II, the Russian Army developed a field expedient tactic to counter the threat posed by German tanks by strapping bombs to starving dogs. In effect, the dogs had been trained to retrieve food from under Russian tanks with the idea that they would then dash under the German tanks seeking food, and in doing so activate a large wooden trigger on their backs. The end result was that this inexpensive weapon system was credited with the destruction of over 300 German tanks. Unfortunately, however, on occasion, some of the dogs having been trained using Russian tanks, demonstrated a penchant for running under Soviet tanks while some others, because of the noise and confusion of the battlefield, ran amok and thus endangered both friend and foe alike.

MAXIM #2
IF IT APPEARS STUPID BUT WORKS, IT ISN'T STUPID

Rochester Castle, England

At the 1215 siege of Rochester Castle, King John ordered the fat from forty pigs to be used to set fire to the new mines beneath the keep, which caused it to collapse, a cheap and effective sapper technique he used in preference to the more complicated mixture of sulfur, tallow, gum, pitch and quicksilver he had used in France the previous year. Animal fat was not uncommon as an accelerant; in the 13th century French sortie-parties would often be equipped with animal fat, straw and flax to use as fuel when setting fires amongst enemy siege engines.

Other incendiary ingredients included egg yolks and pigeon and sheep droppings. Live insects were also used, to sting the enemy. 4th century BC writer Aeneas Tacticus suggested defenders should let wasps and bees into enemy mines, and jars of scorpions were sometimes fired during early bombardment in naval battles.

In 189 BC Ambracia was besieged by the Romans, who dug mines under the walls. The defenders filled a clay jar with chicken feathers, which they then lit, using bellows to blow the acrid smoke down the tunnel; unable to approach the pot due to defensive spears, the Romans were forced to abandon their workings.

In 266 BC, the Greek city of Megara fended off the Macedonian conqueror Antigonus II Gonatas using pigs doused in resin. Antigonus' elephants fled in terror from the bacon brigade. Most battles, however, highlighted the serious drawbacks of tactical barbecue. Since the lifespan of flaming pigs is short, their range was well less than 400 feet. Roughly translated, it meant that the enemy pretty much had to be on top of you before the hogs would have any measurable effect. The porcine missiles also lacked a guidance system, which made them woefully inaccurate. Even when directed toward enemy lines, they often ran wherever they pleased, starting fires on their own side.

MAXIM #2

IF IT APPEARS STUPID BUT WORKS, IT ISN'T STUPID

A trebuchet is a siege engine that was used in the Middle Ages. It is sometimes called a counterweight trebuchet or counterpoise trebuchet, to distinguish it from an earlier weapon called the traction trebuchet, which employed pulling men working the mechanism.

The counterweight trebuchet appeared in both Christian and Muslim lands around the Mediterranean in the 12th century. It could fling projectiles weighing up to 350 pounds at or into enemy fortifications. Its use continued into the 15th century, well after the introduction of gunpowder.

Large trebuchet catapults and the Chateau de Castelnaud Castle in the Dordogne River Valley of Perigord, Aquitane, France in Winter

It is believed that the first traction trebuchets were used by the Mohists in China as early as the 5th century BC, descriptions of which can be found in the *Mojing* (compiled in the 4th century BC). The Chinese named the later counterweight trebuchet *Huihui Pao* (Muslim Weapons, *huihui* means Muslim) or *Xiangyang Pao,* where *pao* means bombard.

The traction trebuchet next appeared in Byzantium. The *Strategikon* of Emperor Maurice, composed in the late 6th century, calls for "ballistae revolving in both directions." The *Miracles of St. Demetrius,* composed by John I, archbishop of Thessalonike, clearly describe traction trebuchets in the Avaro-Slav artillery: "Hanging from the back sides of these pieces of timber were slings and from the front strong ropes, by which, pulling down and releasing the sling, they propel the stones up high and with a loud noise." (John I 597 1:154, ed. Lemerle 1979)

They were also used with great effect by the Islamic armies during the Muslim conquests. A surviving Arab technical treatise on these machines is *Kitab Aniq fi al-Manajaniq* ("An Elegant Book on

Trebuchets"), written in 1462 by Yusuf ibn Urunbugha al-Zaradkash. It provides detailed construction and operating information.

There is some doubt as to the exact period in which traction trebuchets, or knowledge of them, reached Scandinavia. The Vikings may have known of them at a very early stage, as the monk Abbo de St. Germain reports on the siege of Paris in his epic *De bello Parisiaco,* dated about 890 AD, that engines of war were used. Another source mentions that Nordic people or "the Norsemen" used engines of war at the siege of Angers as early as 873 AD.

MAXIM #2
IF IT APPEARS STUPID BUT WORKS, IT ISN'T STUPID

Painting of Mongols at the Walls, Vasily Maksimov (1844–1911)

While invading the Tangut kingdom in 1207, Genghis Khan's battle-hardened steppe horsemen suffered a momentary setback when attacking the seemingly impregnable fortifications of the city of Volohai. Recognizing that the application of brute force alone would not suffice in securing this critical objective, he devised a cunning strategy wherein he offered to withdraw his Mongol forces provided that the besieged inhabitants would pay a tribute of 1,000 cats and 1,000 swallows. After the Tangut complied, he, in turn, set them ablaze and released them, thereby setting the city on fire in several hundreds of places. Thus, while the garrison was occupied in fighting the fires, the Mongols breached the walls and vanquished their opponent.

MAXIM #2

IF IT APPEARS STUPID BUT WORKS, IT ISN'T STUPID

An image of David Bushnell's Turtle, the First American Submarine (U.S. Navy)

The first American submarine was invented by David Bushnell in 1776. The one-man vessel submerged by admitting water into the hull and surfaced by pumping it out with a hand pump. It was powered by a pedal-operated propeller and armed with a torpedo consisting of a keg of powder that was designed to attach to the enemy's ship hull and detonated by a time fuse. During the evening of September 7, 1776, the Turtle, operated by Sergeant Ezra Lee, conducted an attack on the British ship HMS Eagle. However, the boring device that was operated from inside the oak-planked Turtle failed to penetrate the target vessel's hull. Although the torpedo never attached itself to the enemy ship, the timer did manage to detonate an hour later, resulting in a spectacular explosion that ultimately compelled the British to move their ships farther from the harbor.

MAXIM #2

IF IT APPEARS STUPID BUT WORKS, IT ISN'T STUPID

Punji sticks are placed in areas likely to be passed through by enemy troops. The presence of punji sticks is typically camouflaged by natural undergrowth, crops, grass, brush or similar materials. They were often incorporated into various types of traps; for example, a camouflaged pit into which a man might fall.

Punji sticks were also sometimes deployed in the preparation of an ambush. In the preparation of these stakes, the stake itself would be sharpened and, in some cases, rubbed with toxic plants, frogs or even feces, to cause infections in the wounded enemy. Soldiers lying in wait for the enemy to pass would deploy punji sticks in the areas where the surprised enemy might be expected to take cover,

Punji Stick Boobytrap at Chu Chi Tunnels, Vietnam

thus, soldiers diving for cover would impale themselves. In effect, Punji sticks were not necessarily meant to kill the person who stepped on it; rather, they were designed to wound the enemy and slow or halt his unit while the victim was evacuated to a medical facility.

In 1225 the Tran family, who effectively controlled the Vietnamese throne from 1225–1400 are, arguably, best remembered for their defense of the country against the Mongols. By 1225, the Mongols controlled most of northern China and Manchuria but were eyeing southern China, Vietnam, and Champa. In 1257, 1284, and 1287, the Mongol armies of Kublai Khan invaded Vietnam, sacking the capital at Thang Long (renamed Hanoi in 1831) on each occasion, only to find that the Vietnamese had anticipated their attacks and evacuated the city beforehand. Disease, shortage of supplies, the climate, and the Vietnamese strategy of harassment and scorched earth tactics foiled the first two invasions. The third Mongol invasion, of 300,000 men and a vast fleet, was also defeated by the Vietnamese under the leadership of General Tran Hung Dao at the Battle of Back Đằng (1288). Borrowing a tactic used by Ngo Quyen in 938 to defeat an invading Chinese fleet, the Vietnamese drove iron-tipped stakes into the bed of the Bach Dang River and then, with a small Vietnamese flotilla, lured the Mongol fleet into the river just as the tide was starting to ebb. Trapped or impaled by the iron-tipped stakes, the entire Mongol fleet of 400 craft was sunk, captured, or burned by Vietnamese fire arrows and Omar, the Mongolian fleet admiral, was captured and executed. The Mongol army then retreated to China, while being harassed enroute by Tran Hung Dao's troops.

MAXIM #2
IF IT APPEARS STUPID BUT WORKS, IT ISN'T STUPID

Statue of the Cid, in Burgos, Spain

El Cid: People of Valencia! I bring you bread!

Rodrigo Diaz de Bivar was born in 1043 AD and died in 1099. His name, "El Cid" was given to him by the Moors (meaning lord or chief) and he was mainly known for his conquest of the Moors at the siege of Valencia in 1094.

Valencia was one of the largest and richest cities in Moorish Spain. It was strongly fortified, but El Cid was determined to attack it. The plain about the city was irrigated by streams that came down from the neighboring hills. To prevent the Cid's army from coming near the city, the Saracens flooded the plain. But the Cid camped on high ground above the plain and from that point besieged the city. Food became very scarce in Valencia. Wheat, barley and cheese were only available for the wealthy and, as such, many people were forced to eat horses, dogs, cats and mice in order to survive. After conducting an 11-month siege, with only three horses and a mule left alive, the governor surrendered the keys to the city to him on June 15, 1094. El Cid then declared himself the Prince of Valencia.

Charlton Heston portrayed Rodrigo Diaz de Bivar in the renowned 1961 movie classic El Cid. While laying siege to Valencia, El Cid executes a brilliant psychological ploy by commanding his troops to catapult a few loaves of bread into the enemy fortress, thereby causing pandemonium amongst the starving, demoralized Saracens who began fighting for the few scraps of food. Ultimately, realizing their pitiful fate, the Saracens surrendered in quick fashion. As Flavius Vegetius Renatus correctly surmised in Military Institutions of the Romans, circa 378 AD, "Famine makes a greater havoc in an army than the enemy and is more terrible than the sword." Fredrick the Great, in his Instructions to His Generals in 1747 also commented in similar fashion that "The greatest secret of war and the masterpiece of a skillful general is to starve his enemy. Hunger exhausts men more surely than courage, and you will succeed with less risk than by fighting."

MAXIM #2

IF IT APPEARS STUPID BUT WORKS, IT ISN'T STUPID

WWI British Mark V Heavy Tank

Major Ernest Dunlop Swinton, while serving as a British official war correspondent in France in 1914, envisioned building an armored tractor with caterpillar tracks to cross difficult terrain and to shield advancing infantry. Subsequent to the failure of the Somme, British commander, Field Marshal Douglas Haig, a trained cavalryman, realized that trench warfare made the use of horse cavalry null and void and saw the potential of this new behemoth weapon to exploit infantry breakthroughs with harassing attacks to the enemy rear. Accordingly, he commissioned the production of 1,000 tanks to help end the stalemate in the trenches. Although the tanks' steel armor proved effective in stopping small arms fires and fragments from high explosive artillery shells, their slow travel pace (usually about a walking pace) made them vulnerable to direct hits from artillery and mortar shells. Further, many tank crews complained that the environment inside was contaminated with poisonous carbon monoxide, fuels and oil vapors from the engine and cordite fumes from the weapons, with temperatures exceeding 120 degrees Fahrenheit, which contributed toward several crews losing consciousness or becoming violently ill when exposed to fresh air.

The first successful use of tanks came in the Battle of Cambrai on November 20, 1917. British Colonel J.F.C. Fuller, Chief of Staff of the Tank Corps, planned the battle. At 0620 hours, covered by a brief barrage from 1000 guns, the tanks of C and F Battalions in MkIV tanks advanced alongside the men of the British 12th Division against the impregnable German Hindenburg line at Cambrai. Supported in the air by four RFC squadron flying ground attack missions, the general offensive had broken through three trench lines and penetrated five miles on a six-mile front by noon. Although these gains were not exploited and later retaken by a German counter offensive, Cambrai showed the full potential of the tank on the battlefield.

MAXIM #2

IF IT APPEARS STUPID BUT WORKS, IT ISN'T STUPID

Nose Cone, Pigeon-Guided Missile

During World War II, American behavioral psychologist/behaviorist B.F. Skinner developed an experimental device that harnessed pigeons' pecking movements to steer missiles, better known as Project Pigeon or later as Project Orcon for "organic control." Skinner divided this nose cone into three compartments and proposed strapping a pigeon in each one. As a bomb headed towards earth, each pigeon would see the target on its screen. By pecking at the image by operant conditioning (one trained bird pecked at an image more than 10,000 times in 45 minutes), the birds would activate a guidance system that would keep the bomb on the right path until impact. Although Skinner's idea received initial support, the U.S. military finally dismissed it as impractical.

BAT BOMB

During World War II, an oral surgeon named Lytle Adams contacted the White House about using bats as a secret weapon. Troops could strap little bombs to bats, airdrop them into Axis strongholds, and watch the destruction from a safe distance. Franklin Roosevelt was intrigued with the concept and authorized testing in 1942. By 1943,

Adams and the U.S. Army had recruited thousands of Mexican free-tailed bats for the job, while Louis Fieser, the inventor of napalm, designed their one-ounce detonating packs. According to plans, a carrier with 26 stacked trays—each containing 40 little bat homes—would parachute into the industrial cities of Japan's Osaka Bay. The bats would then fly off and wedge themselves into the nooks and crannies of buildings to sleep off their jet lag—at least until a timer detonated their packs. Unfortunately, the bats never were released to perform their kamikaze-like mission. During one test run in Carlsbad, New Mexico the bats got loose, roosted under a fuel tank, and incinerated the facility. After both the Army and Navy conceded defeat in implementing the program, the Marines took over and eventually conducted a successful test on a mock Japanese village in Utah.

MAXIM #2

IF IT APPEARS STUPID BUT WORKS, IT ISN'T STUPID

Photo of a Sturmgewehr 44 rifle

This photo depicts a German *Sturmgewehr* 44 (StG44), originally called the *Maschinenkarabiner* 1942 or MKb 42. Early in 1944, Hitler was approached by several commanders from the Eastern

Front, who expressed a crucial need for a more reliable and lethal assault rifle. As such, in July 1944, the *Sturmgewehr* or "storm rifle" was developed and ordered into production with a total of 425,977 StG44s being manufactured by the end of the war. Several attachments were created for this new weapon to include the *Krummlauf*, a bent barrel that permitted firing around corners. These were most commonly made with 30° and 45° bends."

MAXIM #2

IF IT APPEARS STUPID BUT WORKS, IT ISN'T STUPID

Aunt Jemima Incendiary Device

As part of an attempt to supply arms to the Chinese to aid resistance against the Japanese during WWII, George Bogdan Kistiakowsky of the Office of Strategic Services (OSS) developed a homemade incendiary known as 'Aunt Jemima' (the name of a popular brand of American pancake flour). This recipe consisted of a mixture of nitromine high explosive (better known as HMX) with regular baking flour to create a volatile compound that appeared to be an innocuous culinary delight and, as such, was easily trafficked through Japanese check-points to the Chinese resistance-fighters.

Frank Gleason, a master demolitionist and saboteur, observed the following: *In China we made muffins from the stuff. I wanted to show Major Miles how you could bake Aunt Jemima into muffins, put a blasting cap into it, and blow something up. It looks like regular flour, but if you look carefully at a little piece, you'd see it was gritty, unlike flour. It could make bread, so I told this Chinese cook at Happy Valley to make some muffins out of the explosive flour. I said, "Do not eat those muffins! They are poison. Do not eat them!" You should have seen them when they came out of the oven. They were gorgeous. The cook thought to himself, "Those damn Americans just want those muffins for themselves!" He violated what I told him, and he ate one. He almost died.*

After further testing, the compound was refined to yield a less toxic and edible version. The deadly, delicious muffins or pancakes could now be used as a devastating explosive device, *and* a non-vomit-inducing snack. Uneaten pancakes or unused dough could still be used later for its original explosive purposes. In China during WWII, 15 tons of Aunt Jemima was used, and none was ever discovered by the Japanese.

MAXIM #2

IF IT APPEARS STUPID BUT WORKS, IT ISN'T STUPID

Tallboy Bomb

The **Tallboy** or **Bomb, Medium Capacity, 12,000 lb**, was an earthquake bomb developed by the British aeronautical engineer Barnes Wallis and deployed by the RAF in 1944. It weighed five tons and, carried by the Avro Lancaster, was effective against hardened structures against which earlier, smaller bombs had proven ineffective.

Barnes Wallis presented his ideas for a 10-ton bomb in his 1941 paper *A Note on a Method of Attacking the Axis Powers*, which showed that a very large bomb exploding deep underground next to a target would transmit the shock into the foundations of the target, particularly since shock waves are transmitted through the ground more strongly than through air.

Wallis designed the "Victory Bomber" of 50 tons, which would fly at 320 mph at 45,000 feet to carry the heavy bomb over 4,000 miles but the Air Ministry was against a single-bomb aircraft, and the idea was not pursued beyond 1942.

Following Wallis' 1942 paper *Spherical Bomb — Surface Torpedo* and the design of the "bouncing bomb" for the Dam Busters of Operation Chastise, the design and production of Tallboy was done without a contract on the initiative of the Ministry. As such, the RAF was using bombs they had not bought and that were still the property of the manufacturer, Vickers. This situation was normalized once their capabilities were recognized.

Accomplishments of the Tallboy included the 24 June, 1944 Operation Crossbow attack on La Coupole — along with Grand Slams — which undermined the foundations of the V-2 assembly bunker, and a Tallboy attack on the Saumur tunnel on June 8-9, 1944, when bombs passed straight through the hill and exploded inside the tunnel 60 feet below the surface.

The last of the Kriegsmarine's *Bismarck*-class battleships, the *Tirpitz*, was sunk by an air attack using Tallboys.

MAXIM #2
IF IT APPEARS STUPID BUT WORKS, IT ISN'T STUPID

Young Boy modeling Ancient Chinese Armor

Paper Armor

Zhijia, or paper armor, originated during the Tang dynasty during the reign of Tangyizong (859 – 873 AD) and was designed as a cost-effective measure to protect the troops since traditional metal and leather armor was a luxury that only noblemen and elite troops could afford.

The actual construction of the armor was extremely cheap to produce since it merely consisted of a form of processed paper typically ranging from one to three inches in thickness. Under wet conditions such as rain, the material would harden, thus making it a valuable form of defense against arrows. Yet another tactical advantage was that paper armor, unlike metal armor, did not rust and its lightness and flexible nature allowed for the greatest form of mobility; especially in the southern campaigns where there were large amounts of rivers and forests to contend with.

Some noteworthy examples where paper armor was successfully used was during the Song-Hsia wars where over thirty thousand besieged archers of the Song Dynasty were outfitted with this type of armor while defending the fortress of Shanxi and during General Qi Jiguang's campaign against the Japanese pirates, wherein a large number of his troops wore this form of armor since it proved effective against the firearms of the time.

MAXIM #2

LESSON LEARNED

Necessity is truly the mother of invention and when confronted with desperate circumstances there is no limit to the enemy's ingenuity in devising a destructive weapon.

Ridiculously Oversized Punt Gun Photo

MAXIM #3

IF YOUR ATTACK IS GOING REALLY WELL, IT'S AN AMBUSH

Mongol warriors, miniature from Rashīd al-Dīn's History of the World, 1307; in the Edinburgh University Library, Scotland

The Mongols commonly practiced the feigned retreat, which is perhaps the most difficult battlefield tactic to execute. This is because a feigned rout amongst untrained troops can often turn into a real rout if the enemy presses into it. Pretending disarray and defeat in the heat of the battle, the Mongols would suddenly appear panicked and turn and run, only to pivot when the enemy was drawn out, destroying them at their own leisure. Once this feigned retreat became known to the enemy, the Mongols would extend the feigned retreat for days or weeks, to falsely convince the chasers that they were defeated and only to charge back once the enemy had their guards down or had retreated to join their main formation.

In May 1222, the Mongol generals Jebe and Sube'etei and 20,000 Mongol cavalrymen pursued the fleeing Kypchaks (or Cumans) from the western side of the Caspian Sea toward the northwest to Kiev. The Mongols met the joint forces of the Russians and the Cumans, 30,000 men, on the eastern bank of the Dnieper River. Some say that Sube'etei, with only 2,000 Mongol cavalry, lured the Russians and Cumans for nine days toward the small Kalka River that flows into the Sea of Azov, where the main Mongol cavalrymen (numbering 20,000) were waiting. Under the direction of Jebe and Sube'etei, the Mongols attacked the enemy at the end of May and destroyed most of their forces.

MAXIM #3
IF YOUR ATTACK IS GOING REALLY WELL, IT'S AN AMBUSH

Hannibal Barca counting the rings of the Roman Knights killed at the Battle of Cannae, for Versailles 1704 Tuileries Garden Louveres Museum

Battle of Cannae August 2, 216 BC, 2nd Punic War – Hannibal, commanding an army of roughly 40,000 heavy infantry, 6,000 light infantry and 10,000 cavalry, decisively defeated a numerically superior army of the Roman Republic consisting of 80,000 infantry, 2,400 Roman cavalry and 4,000 allied horse who were jointly commanded by the cautious military veteran and patrician consul, Lucius Aemilius Paullus, and the egomaniacal and inept plebian consul, Gais Terrentius Varro. During this campaign to quash the Carthaginian army, the command of the Roman army alternated each day between the consuls and, accordingly, Hannibal opted to engage the Romans when it was commanded by the inexperienced, amateur General Varro. More specifically, Hannibal, cognizant that Varro was suspicious of his past victories that relied on trickery and ruses, deliberately deployed his Carthaginian troops in a crescent formation with their backs to the Aufidus River, gambling that Varro would now be tempted to attack him by virtue that the likelihood of an ambush was remote on an open field and, moreover, that his position so close to the river would measurably limit his ability to maneuver his troops and thus allow the Romans to press their advantage of superior numbers by frontally assaulting the center of the Carthaginian line that was mainly comprised of inexperienced Iberian, Gaul and Cetiberian infantryman. Initially, the overzealous Varro succeeded in pushing back the weak Carthaginian center, but this was merely a brilliant ruse. In effect, Hannibal intended that his cavalry, consisting of mainly of medium Hispanic cavalry and Numidian light horse, and positioned on the flanks, would defeat the weaker Roman cavalry and eventually swing around to attack the Roman infantry from the rear as it pressed upon Hannibal's weakened center that was falling back in orderly fashion. His veteran African troops would then press in from the flanks at the crucial moment and encircle the overextended Roman army, who would be so tightly compacted that they would have little space to wield their weapons. Ultimately, according to Livy the historian, in a few short, bloody hours, Hannibal's audacious tactic of double envelopment with a numerically inferior army resulted in the deaths of approximately

45,500 foot soldiers and 2,700 horsemen and he also reports that 3,000 Roman and allied infantry and 1,500 Roman and allied cavalry were taken prisoner by the Carthaginians. In closing, the Battle of Cannae is therefore regarded as one of the greatest tactical defeats in military history and the second greatest defeat of Rome (second only to the Battle of Arausio in 105 BC) and is taught in military academies as the apogee of the general's art.

MAXIM #3

IF YOUR ATTACK IS GOING REALLY WELL, IT'S AN AMBUSH

Painting Title: Custer's Last Stand by Edgar S. Paxson (1852–1919)

LTC Custer – "Hurrah boys, we've got them! We'll finish them and then go home to our station" as reported by SGT Charles Windolph in his book entitled "I Fought with Custer"

The Battle of the Little Bighorn —also known as Custer's Last Stand—was an armed engagement between a Lakota-Northern Cheyenne combined force and the 7th Calvary Regiment of the United States Army. It occurred on June 25 and June 26, 1876, near the Little Bighorn River in the eastern Montana Territory.

The battle was an overwhelming victory for the Lakota and Northern Cheyenne, led by Chief Sitting Bull. The U.S. Seventh Cavalry, including a column of 700 men led by George Armstrong Custer, suffered a severe defeat. Five of the Seventh's companies were annihilated; Custer was killed, as were two of his brothers, a nephew, and a brother-in-law. Total US deaths were 268, including scouts, and 55 were wounded.

Custer's scouts warned him about the size of the village, with scout Mitch Bouyer reportedly saying, "General, I have been with these Indians for 30 years, and this is the largest village I have ever heard of." Custer's overriding concern was that the Native American group would break up and scatter in different directions, so he pressed his attack, only to discover that the Indians marshaled a force of 1,800 warriors; i.e. a 3-1 advantage.

MAXIM #3
LESSON LEARNED

Don't let your ego dictate your tactics and strategy. Know your enemy and yourself and understand that all warfare is based upon deception – Sun Tzu

Terracotta Warriors of Qin Shi Huang, the First Emperor of China located in Lintong District, Xi`an, Shaanxi

MAXIM #4

NEVER SHARE A FOXHOLE WITH ANYONE BRAVER THAN YOURSELF & FAMOUS LAST STANDS

Illustration by John Steeple Davis – (1841–1917)

The **Battle of Thermopylae** was fought between an alliance of Greek city-states, led by King Leonidas of Sparta, and the Persian Empire of Xerxes I over the course of three days, during the second Persian invasion of Greece. It took place simultaneously with the naval battle at Artemisium, in August 480 BC, at the narrow coastal pass of Thermopylae ('The Hot Gates'). The Persian invasion was a delayed response to the defeat of the first Persian invasion of Greece, which had been ended by the Athenian victory at the Battle of Marathon in 490 BC. Xerxes had amassed a huge army and navy and set out to conquer all of Greece. The Athenian general Themistocles had proposed that the allied Greeks block the advance of the Persian army at the pass of Thermopylae, and simultaneously block the Persian navy at the Straits of Artemisium.

A Greek force of approximately 7,000 men marched north to block the pass in the summer of 480 BC. The Persian army, alleged by the ancient sources to have numbered over one million but today considered to have been much smaller (various figures are given by scholars ranging between about 70,000 to 300,000), arrived at the pass on August 18. The vastly outnumbered Greeks held off the Persians for seven days (including three days of battle) and inflicted approximately 20,000 casualties before the rearguard was annihilated in one of history's most famous last stands.

MAXIM #4

NEVER SHARE A FOXHOLE WITH ANYONE BRAVER THAN YOURSELF & FAMOUS LAST STANDS

The Battle of Thermopylae continued:

During two full days of battle the small force led by King Leonidas I of Sparta blocked the only road by which the massive Persian army could pass. After the second day of battle, a local resident named Ephialtes of Trachis betrayed the Greeks by revealing a small hidden goat path named Anopaea Pass that led behind the Greek lines. Leonidas, aware that his force was being outflanked, dismissed the bulk of the Greek army and remained to guard the rear with 300 Spartans, 700 Thespians, 400 Thebans and perhaps a few hundred others, most of whom were killed.

For three days they held out between two narrow cliff faces to prevent the use of Xerxes' vast cavalry and infantry force before being outflanked on the third day via the hidden goat path that Ephialtes identified to the Persians.

Shortly thereafter, a Persian emissary was sent by Xerxes to negotiate with Leonidas. The Greeks were offered their freedom and the title "Friends of the Persian People," and, moreover, they would be re-settled on land better than that they possessed. When these terms were refused by Leonidas, the ambassador asked him more forcefully to lay down his weapons. Leonidas' famous response to the Persian emissary was *"Molon Labe,"* which roughly translates to "Come and take them!" After repeated efforts to explain to the Spartans the futility of their predicament, the exasperated negotiator then asserted that "Our arrows will block out the sun," to which one of Leonidas' subordinates, Dienekes, rejoined, "Then we shall have our battle in the shade!"

With the Persian embassy returning empty-handed, battle became inevitable. Xerxes delayed for four days, waiting for the Greeks to disperse, before sending troops to attack them.

Simonides' Epitaph at the Thermopylae monument: "Go tell the Spartans, stranger passing by, that here obedient to their laws we lie."

Leonidas Monument at Thermopylae, Greece

MAXIM #4

NEVER SHARE A FOXHOLE WITH ANYONE BRAVER THAN YOURSELF & FAMOUS LAST STANDS

A view from Arbel Valley to the south on the Ridge of Horns of Hattin, where Salah a-din beat the Crusaders
Battle of Hattin – June 1187 – The Second Crusade

An entire Christian army is slaughtered when it stops for a drink of water.

The battle took place near Tiberias (now known as the Sea of Galilee in present-day Israel). The battlefield, near the town of

Hattin, had as its main geographic feature two hills (the "Horns of Hattin") beside a pass through the northern mountains between Tiberias and the road from Acre to the west. The Darb al-Hawarnah road, built by the Romans, served as the main east-west passage between the Jordan fords, the Sea of Galilee and the Mediterranean coast.

Prelude:

On May 1, 1187, Sultan Saladin, the Muslim/Saracen commander, seeking revenge for a treacherous attack on a Muslim caravan by Raynald of Châtillon, who violated the Armistice of 1183, dispatched a small raiding party of approximately 700 soldiers to attack approximately 130 Knights Templars & Hospitallers, 400 infantrymen and an unknown number of "*turcopoles*" (mounted archers/ light cavalry) at the springs of Cresson. The Muslims virtually annihilated the Crusaders and only the Grand Master of the Knights Templar, Gerard of Ridefort, and three knights managed to escape. The Islamic invaders then rode back to Syria across Galilee, displaying the heads of the Crusaders who had been killed in battle on the point of their lances.

MAXIM #4

NEVER SHARE A FOXHOLE WITH ANYONE BRAVER THAN YOURSELF & FAMOUS LAST STANDS

Prelude continued:

Saladin, emboldened by the successful attack at Cresson and wanting to further exploit the political feud between Count Raymond

III of Tripoli (the former regent of Jerusalem) and the French Crusader Knight Guy of Lusignan (the brother-in-law and successor of the recently deceased leper King Baldwin IV and Baldwin's young nephew and heir) recruited a force of 30,000 soldiers and 12,000 regular cavalry troops and then crossed the Jordan River on June 30, 1187 to destroy the Crusader army once and for all.

The barons of the realm, desperate to counter the impending Islamic threat, beseeched Raymond to reconcile with King Guy and the two ultimately met at the Saint Job fortress. After amassing a force of approximately 20,000 soldiers that also included 1,200 knights from Jerusalem and Tripoli and another 50 from Antioch, the Crusader army, along with the relic of the True Cross, carried by the Bishop of Acre, the Crusaders marched to meet Saladin's forces.

The Attack:

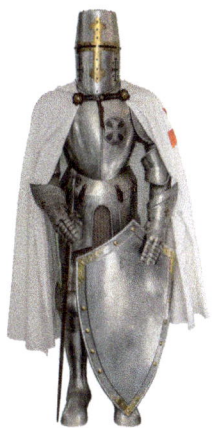

Templar Knight, Battle of Hattin – June 1187 – The Second Crusade

On July 2, 1187 Saladin's scouts reported that Guy's army was seen at the springs of Sephoria, the last substantial water reserve before Lake Tiberias. Wanting to lure Guy to moving the main army away from the springs so that he could ultimately engage them on open ground, Saladin personally led a siege of Raymond's fortress at Tiberias while his main force remained at Kafr Sabt. The outmanned garrison, realizing its dire predicament, attempted to bribe Saladin into withdrawing his forces, but the ploy proved unsuccessful since Saladin would not be tricked or contented with tribute. After his sappers breached the tower, the Muslim force killed most of the defenders and captured Raymond's wife Eschiva. The other survivors were then sold into slavery.

MAXIM #4

NEVER SHARE A FOXHOLE WITH ANYONE BRAVER THAN YOURSELF & FAMOUS LAST STANDS

The Attack continued:

On July 3rd, Guy ordered the army on a forced march against Saladin and, while enroute to relieve the besieged garrison at Tiberias, failed to rest his army at the Springs of Turan. Throughout the entire march, the Crusader army was harassed by Muslim archers and the troops became increasingly despondent and tormented by thirst. Count Raymond, leading the vanguard element and realizing that his forces would not reach Tiberias by the evening, prompted Guy to change course to march to the Springs of Kafr Hattin, which was only a few hours' march.

The Muslims, upon witnessing the course change, brilliantly positioned themselves between the Crusaders and the water source and Raymond and Guy were eventually forced to pitch camp that night on an arid plateau near the village of Meskana.

On the morning of July 4th, Guy's army awoke to blinding smoke created by fires set by Saladin's men to screen their actions

A Crusader knight charging the enemy

and to, moreover, increase the misery of the Crusaders who hadn't had any water for over a day. Despite having sufficient numbers to break through the Muslim lines, thirsty and demoralized, the Crusaders broke camp to reach the springs of Hattin, but their ragged approach was continually attacked by Saladin's army, which continued to block the route forward as well as any possible retreat.

Raymond then launched two charges in an attempt to break through to the other water supply source at Lake Tiberias. Unfortunately, both charges failed, and he became cut off from the main army and forced to retreat.

After Raymond escaped, Guy's position now became even more precarious. Most of the Crusader infantry had effectively deserted by moving on to the Horns of Hattin in order to escape the storm of destruction. Guy then attempted to pitch the tents again to block the Muslim cavalry, but without infantry protection the knights' horses were cut down by Muslim archers and the cavalry was forced to fight on foot and to retreat to the Horns to support the infantry.

MAXIM #4

NEVER SHARE A FOXHOLE WITH ANYONE BRAVER THAN YOURSELF & FAMOUS LAST STANDS

The Attack continued:

Guy's exhausted army, despite launching three desperate and heroic charges on Saladin's position, were eventually defeated and ultimately brought to Saladin's tent, whereupon Guy was given a goblet of iced rosewater as a sign of Saladin's generosity. When Guy passed the goblet to his fellow captive Reynald de Chatillon, Saladin allowed the old, treacherous knight to drink but shortly afterwards said that he had not offered water to Reynald and thus was not bound by the Muslim rules of hospitality. When Saladin accused Reynald of being an oath breaker, Reynald replied, "Kings have always acted thus. I did nothing more." Saladin then executed Reynald by beheading him with his sword. Guy fell to his knees at the sight of Reynald's corpse, but Saladin bade him rise, saying, "It is not the wont of kings to kill kings; but that man had transgressed all bounds, and therefore did I treat him thus. This man was only killed because of his malfeasance and perfidy."

Aftermath:

Precise casualties for the battle are not known, but it resulted in the destruction of the majority of the Crusader army and 3,000 Franks escaping the battlefield. Saladin commanded that Guy, the other captive Frankish barons and the Grand Master of the Temple were to be spared and treated humanely since they ultimately would be ransomed. The remaining common soldiers were sold into slavery. However, as for the fate of the remaining 200 Templar and Hospitaller Knights, they were summarily beheaded.

With respect to the fate of the True Cross that the Bishop of Acre carried in battle to boost the morale of the Crusader army, the Muslims supposedly fixed it upside down on a lance and then sent it to Damascus.

On July 5th, Saladin traveled to Tiberias, whereupon Countess Eschiva surrendered the citadel of the fortress. She, along with her family, was allowed to leave for Tripoli. As for Count Raymond, who had escaped the battle, he later died of pleurisy shortly thereafter.

Quickly advancing in the wake of his victory, Saladin captured Acre, Nablus, Jaffa, Toron, Sidon, Beirut, and Ascalon in rapid succession. Moving against Jerusalem that September, it was surrendered by Balian on October 2. The defeat at Hattin, according to the chronicler Ernoul, caused Pope Urban III to die of shock and ultimately led to the Third Crusade of the Holy Land being waged in 1189, with troops commanded by Richard the Lionheart and Frederick I.

MAXIM #4

NEVER SHARE A FOXHOLE WITH ANYONE BRAVER THAN YOURSELF & FAMOUS LAST STANDS

Aerial Photo of Masada Fortress, Israel – January 3, 2012

Masada is an ancient fortification in the Southern District of Israel, situated on top of an isolated rock plateau on the eastern edge of the Judaean Desert and which overlooks the Dead Sea. Herod the Great built palaces for himself on the mountain and fortified Masada between 37 and 31 BC.

In 66 AD, a group of Jewish rebels, the Sicarii (referred to by the Jewish-Roman historian Josephus as an extremist Jewish splinter group antagonistic to a larger group of rebellious Jews referred to as the Zealots), overcame the Roman garrison of Masada with the aid of a ruse and shortly thereafter with the destruction of the Second Temple in 70 AD, additional members of the Sicarii fled Jerusalem and settled on the mountaintop.

In 73 AD, the Roman governor of Judaea, Lucius Flavius Silva – Commander of Roman Legion X *Fretensis*) deployed approximately

15,000 troops (which also consisted of several auxiliary units and Jewish prisoners of war) to crush the Jewish resistance at Masada. Despite the daunting challenge of attacking this fortress on very difficult terrain (the east edge of Masada is about 1,300 feet high and the cliffs on the west are about 300 feet high), his Roman engineers built a 375-foot-high assault ramp consisting mostly of a natural spur of bedrock and then labored to move a giant siege tower with a battering ram against the western face of the plateau. On April 16, after a three-month siege, the Romans finally breached the fortress walls.

According to Josephus, when Roman troops entered the fortress, they discovered that its 960 inhabitants had set all the buildings with the food storerooms ablaze and committed mass suicide by killing each other. Only two women and five children were found alive.

MAXIM #4
NEVER SHARE A FOXHOLE WITH ANYONE BRAVER THAN YOURSELF & FAMOUS LAST STANDS

The **Battle of Jacob's Ford** was a victory of the Muslim Sultan Saladin over the Christian King of Jerusalem, Baldwin IV. It occurred in August 1179, when Saladin conquered and destroyed a new border castle built by the Knights Templar at Jacob's Ford on the upper River Jordan, a historic passage point between the Golan Heights and northern Galilee.

Between October 1178 and April 1179, King Baldwin began the first stages of constructing his new line of defense, a fortification called Chastellet at Jacob's Ford. While construction was in progress,

Krak des Chevaliers Crusader Castle, Syria

Saladin became fully aware of the task he would have to overcome at Jacob's Ford if he were to protect Syria and conquer Jerusalem. At the time, he was unable to stop the erection of Chastellet by military force because a large portion of his troops were stationed in northern Syria, putting down Muslim rebellions. As one author writes, "Saladin was always at pains to portray himself as the champion of Islam against the European intruders, although in fact he spent much, if not more, of his career involved in a war against… other Muslims." Consequently, the sultan turned to bribery and offered Baldwin 60,000 dinars to halt construction. Baldwin declined, but Saladin then made a counter-offer of 100,000 dinars. The Christian king refused again and continued to build Chastellet. By the summer of 1179, Baldwin's forces had constructed a stone wall of massive proportions. "The castle now had a formidable ten-meter-high wall – what one Arabic contemporary later described as 'an impregnable rampart of stone and iron' – and a single tower, but it was still a work in progress."

Saladin, after having both bribes rejected, then summoned a large Muslim army to lay siege to the castle and its inhabitants before any reinforcements from Jerusalem or any of its neighboring territories could arrive. On August 30, Saladin's army ultimately proved successful in seizing the fort and killed 700 Crusaders and then threw them in a pit, where they decayed in the summer heat.

MAXIM #4

NEVER SHARE A FOXHOLE WITH ANYONE BRAVER THAN YOURSELF & FAMOUS LAST STANDS

Crusader at the Battle of Acre

Siege of Acre – The Third Crusade

The **Siege of Acre** was one of the first confrontations of the Third Crusade lasting from August 28, 1189 until July 12, 1191, and the deadliest event of the whole period of the Crusades for the Christian ruling class of the East. During the siege, Saladin collected money to pay King Richard the ransom of the imprisoned

Muslim garrison. Despite Saladin's efforts to deliver the first of three planned payments and prisoner exchanges, Richard rejected his offer because certain Christian nobles were not included. When further negotiations proved unsuccessful on August 20, 1191, King Richard, believing that Saladin lacked the requisite sense of urgency to bring the matter to resolution, decapitated 2,700 Muslim prisoners from the garrison of Acre. Saladin then responded in kind by killing all the Christian prisoners he captured.

MAXIM #4

NEVER SHARE A FOXHOLE WITH ANYONE BRAVER THAN YOURSELF & FAMOUS LAST STANDS

The Sack of Rome in front of the Castle Sant'Angelo, Vatican City, Rome, Italy

The **Stand of the Swiss Guard** took place during the sacking of Rome on May 6, 1527, when the Pope's Swiss guards held off troops loyal to the Habsburgs long enough for Pope Clement to escape.

The Habsburg army, composed of Imperial and Spanish troops, was placed under the command of the Constable of France, the Duc de Bourbon, fallen from grace in France and now serving the enemy. The constable's army, with a large contingent of Lutheran mercenaries, had become increasingly mutinous, and the Emperor was preoccupied with other matters, making him unable to pay them.

Because of his troops' attitudes, Bourbon decided to attack Rome, known to be filled with potential loot. The city, considered to be the inviolable capital of Christendom, was left almost defenseless, and, when the Pope anxiously ordered the citizens to take up arms, only 500 obeyed. Bourbon's troops quickly overwhelmed the defenders and began to plunder the ancient city. Near St. Peter's Basilica, the Swiss Guard, as the Pope's elite bodyguard unit, deployed. The Captain, Kaspar Röist, intended to hold off the attackers long enough for Clement to escape across the Passetto di Borgo. Joined by remnants of the Roman garrison, a total of 189 Swiss Guards made their stand in a cemetery well within the Vatican. Captain Röist was wounded and then killed by Spanish mercenaries, in full view of his wife. The Swiss fought bitterly but were heavily outnumbered and almost annihilated. Some survivors, accompanied by a band of refugees, retreated to the Basilica steps. Those who fled toward the Basilica were massacred, and only 42 survived. This group, under the command of Hercules Goldli, managed to stave off the Habsburg troops pursuing the Pope's entourage as it made its way across the Passetto to the Castel Sant'Angelo.

After the city's sack and the Guards' stand, Rome was subjected to a brief occupation, during which Catholic and Lutheran German troops committed outrages against the population and its religious monuments. Pope Clement, from his nominal confinement in the Castel St. Angelo, was forced to listen to cries of "Long live Luther, pontiff!" The Pope was allowed to incorporate the surviving Swiss into his new, Habsburg-authorized guard, but the Swiss Guard was reinstalled in its entirety after the occupation.

MAXIM #4

NEVER SHARE A FOXHOLE WITH ANYONE BRAVER THAN YOURSELF & FAMOUS LAST STANDS

The **Battle of the Alamo** (February 23–March 6, 1836) was a pivotal event in the Texas Revolution. Following a 13-day siege, Mexican troops under President General Antonio López de Santa Anna launched an assault on the Alamo Mission near San Antonio de Béxar (modern-day San Antonio, Texas, USA). All the Texian defenders were killed. Santa Anna's perceived cruelty during the battle inspired many Texians—both Texas settlers and adventurers from the United States—to join the Texian army. Buoyed by a desire for revenge, the Texians defeated the Mexican army at the Battle of San Jacinto, on April 21, 1836, ending the revolution.

Houston could not spare the number of men necessary to mount a successful defense. Instead, he sent Colonel James Bowie with 30 men to remove the artillery from the Alamo and destroy the complex. Bowie was unable to transport the artillery, since the Alamo garrison lacked the necessary draft animals. Neill soon persuaded Bowie that the location held strategic importance. In a letter to Governor Henry Smith, Bowie argued that "the salvation of Texas depends in great measure on keeping Béxar out of the hands of the enemy. It serves as the frontier picquet guard, and if it were in the possession of Santa Anna, there is no stronghold from which to repel him in his march toward the Sabine." The letter to Smith ended, "Colonel Neill and myself have come to the solemn resolution that we will rather die in these ditches than give it up to the enemy." Bowie also wrote to the provisional government, asking for "men, money, rifles, and cannon powder." Few reinforcements were authorized; cavalry officer William B. Travis arrived in Béxar with 30 men on February 3. Five days later, a small group of volunteers arrived, including the famous frontiersman and former U.S. Congressman Davy Crockett of Tennessee.

On March 4, the day after his reinforcements arrived, Santa Anna proposed an assault on the Alamo. Many of his senior officers recommended that they wait for two 12-pounder cannons anticipated to arrive on March 7. That evening, a local woman, likely Bowie's cousin-in-law Juana Navarro Alsbury, approached Santa Anna to negotiate a surrender for the Alamo defenders. According to many historians, this visit probably increased Santa Anna's impatience; as historian Timothy Todish noted, "There would have been little glory in a bloodless victory." The following morning, Santa Anna announced to his staff that the assault would take place early on March 6. Santa Anna arranged for troops from

Béxar to be excused from the front lines so that they would not be forced to fight their own families. Legend holds that at some point on March 5, Travis gathered his men and explained that an attack was imminent, and that the Mexican army would prevail. He supposedly drew a line in the ground and asked those willing to die for the Texian cause to cross and stand alongside him; only one man (Moses Rose) was said to have declined. Susannah Dickinson recalled Travis announcing that any men who wished to escape should let it be known and step out of ranks. The last Texian verified to have left the Alamo was James Allen, a courier who carried personal messages from Travis and several of the other men on March 5th.

MAXIM #4

NEVER SHARE A FOXHOLE WITH ANYONE BRAVER THAN YOURSELF & FAMOUS LAST STANDS

Pierre Cambronne served as a Major of the Imperial Guard in 1814, and accompanied Napoléon into exile to the island of Elba, where he was a military commander. He then returned with Napoléon to France on March 1, 1815 for the Hundred Days, capturing the fortress of Sisteron (5 March), and was made a Count by Napoléon when they arrived at Paris. Cambronne was seriously wounded at the Battle of Waterloo and was taken prisoner by the British.

The exact circumstances of his surrender to the British are disputed. At the battle's conclusion, Cambronne was commanding the last of the Old Guard when General Colville called on him to surrender. According to a journalist named Rougement, Cambronne replied: "*La garde meurt et ne se rend pas!*" (The Guard dies and does not surrender!).

Statue of Brigadier General Pierre Jacques Étienne Cambronne

Retreating French Soldiers

MAXIM #4

NEVER SHARE A FOXHOLE WITH ANYONE BRAVER THAN YOURSELF & FAMOUS LAST STANDS

French Foreign Legion Captain Jean Danjou, Hero of the Battle of Camarón

The Battle of Camarón occurred April 30, 1863 between the French Foreign Legion and the Mexican army. It is regarded by the Legion as a defining moment in the Foreign Legion's history.

A small infantry patrol led by Captain Jean Danjou, numbering 62 soldiers and three officers, was attacked and besieged by a force that eventually reached 3,000 Mexican infantry and cavalry and was forced to make a defensive stand at the nearby Hacienda Camarón, Veracruz, Mexico.

While his legionnaires prepared to defend the inn, the Mexican commander, Colonel Francisco de Paula Milán, demanded that Danjou and his soldiers surrender, noting the Mexican army's numeric superiority. Danjou replied: "We have munitions. We will not surrender." He then swore to fight to the death, an oath which was seconded by the men. A few hours later, Captain Danjou was shot in the chest and died; his soldiers continued fighting despite overwhelming odds under the command of an inspired 2nd Lt. Vilain, who held for four hours before falling during an assault. At approximately 5 p.m. only 12 Legionnaires remained around 2nd Lt. Maudet. Soon after by 6 p.m., with ammunition exhausted, the last of Danjou's soldiers, numbering only five under the command of Lt. Maudet, desperately mounted a bayonet charge. Two men died outright, while the rest continued the assault. The tiny group was surrounded. A Belgian Legionnaire, Victor Catteau, leapt in front of Lt. Maudet to protect him from the Mexican guns when they were leveled at him but died in vain, as both he and Lt. Maudet were hit in the barrage.

When the last two survivors were asked to surrender, they insisted that Mexican soldiers allow them safe passage home, to keep their arms, and to escort the body of Captain Danjou. The Mexican commander then rejoined, "What can I refuse to such men? No, these are not men, they are devils," and, out of respect, agreed to their terms.

MAXIM #4

NEVER SHARE A FOXHOLE WITH ANYONE BRAVER THAN YOURSELF & FAMOUS LAST STANDS

The **Battle of Isandlwana** on January 22, 1879 was the first major encounter in the Anglo–Zulu War between the British Empire and the Zulu Kingdom. Eleven days after the British commenced their invasion of Zululand in South Africa, a Zulu force of some 20,000 warriors attacked a portion of the British main column consisting of about 1,800 British, colonial and native troops and perhaps 400

Sandlwana hill or Sphinx with soldiers graves in foreground, the scene of the Anglo Zulu battle site of January 22, 1879. The great Battlefield of Isandlwana and the Oskarber, Zululand, northern Kwazulu Natal, South Africa

civilians. The Zulus were equipped mainly with the traditional assegai iron spears and cow-hide shields, but also had a number of muskets and old rifles, though they were not formally trained in their use. The British and colonial troops were armed with the state-of-the-art Martini-Henry breech-loading rifles and two 7 pounder artillery pieces as well as a rocket battery. Despite a vast disadvantage in weapons technology, the numerically superior Zulus ultimately overwhelmed the poorly led and badly deployed British, killing over 1,300 troops, including all those out on the forward firing line. The Zulu army suffered approximately a thousand killed.

The battle was a decisive victory for the Zulus and caused the defeat of the first British invasion of Zululand. The British army had suffered its worst defeat against a technologically inferior indigenous force. Isandlwana resulted in the British taking a much more aggressive approach in the Anglo–Zulu War, leading to a heavily reinforced second invasion and the destruction of King Cetshwayo's hopes of a negotiated peace.

MAXIM #4

NEVER SHARE A FOXHOLE WITH ANYONE BRAVER THAN YOURSELF & FAMOUS LAST STANDS

The Last Samurai Saigo Takamori, Tokyo, Japan

Following defeat at the Siege of Kumamoto Castle and in other battles in central Kyūshū, the surviving remnants of the *samurai* forces loyal to Saigō Takamori fled back to Satsuma, seizing the hill of Shiroyama overlooking Kagoshima on September 1, 1877.

Imperial army troops under the command of General Yamagata Aritomo and marines under the command of Admiral Kawamura Sumiyoshi began arriving soon after, and the rebels were surrounded. After combat losses and defections, Saigō had only 300 to 400 *samurai* remaining of a force of over 20,000 which had besieged the government garrison in the city of Kumamoto only six weeks earlier.

With 30,000 troops Yamagata greatly outnumbered Saigō. Having been outfought and outmaneuvered so often in the past, however, Yamagata was determined to leave nothing to chance. The imperial troops spent several days constructing an elaborate system of ditches, walls and obstacles to prevent another breakout.

The five government warships in Kagoshima harbor added their firepower to Yamagata's artillery and began to systematically reduce the rebel positions, firing more than 7,000 shells.

Saigō defended his position with limited musket support, and no cannon. Saigō's force was reduced to melting down metal statuettes that local civilians smuggled in and casting the metal into bullets. Medical supplies consisted of one carpenter's saw for amputations and a few rags for bandages. Yamagata sent a letter to Saigō, which entreated him to surrender, but *bushido* honor would not let Saigō allow it.

Yamagata's battle plan was to assault Saigō's position from all sides at once. Units were forbidden to assist one another without express permission. If a unit retreated with enemy troops in pursuit, the neighboring units were to fire into the area indiscriminately, killing their own men if necessary, to prevent Saigō from escaping.

Following an intensive artillery bombardment on the night of 24 September, imperial forces stormed the mountain in the early morning hours. The *samurai*, under heavy fire, charged the lines of the imperial army, which had not been trained for close-quarter sword fighting. In just a few minutes the once organized line turned into discord. Highly skilled *samurai* swordsmanship prevailed against an army with very little traditional training. For a short time Saigō's lines held but was forced back due to weight of numbers. By 6 a.m., only 40 rebels were still alive. Saigō was wounded in the femoral artery and stomach. Losing blood rapidly, he asked to find a suitable spot to die. One of his most loyal followers, Beppu Shinsuke, carried him further down the hill on his shoulders. Legend says that Beppu acted as *kaishakunin* and aided Saigō in committing *seppuku* before he could be captured. However, other evidence contradicts this, stating that Saigō, in fact, died of a bullet wound and then had his head removed by Beppu to preserve it. On February 22, 1889, Emperor Meiji pardoned Saigō posthumously.

MAXIM #4

NEVER SHARE A FOXHOLE WITH ANYONE BRAVER THAN YOURSELF & FAMOUS LAST STANDS

U.S. Army 442nd Infantry Regimental Coin

The 442nd Regimental Combat Team of the United States Army was a regimental-size fighting unit comprised almost entirely of American soldiers of Japanese descent who fought in World War II. The 442nd, beginning in 1944, was a self-sufficient force, and fought with uncommon distinction in Italy, southern France, and Germany. The 442nd is considered to be the most decorated infantry regiment in the history of the United States Army. More specifically the 442nd was awarded 8 Presidential Unit Citations, 21 Medal of Honors, 52 Distinguished Service Crosses, 1 Distinguished Service Medal, 560 Silver Stars + 28 Oak Leaf Clusters for a second award, 22 Legion of Merit Medals, 15 Soldier Medals, 4000 Bronze Stars + 1,200 Oak Leaf Clusters and 9,846 Purple Hearts. The 442nd's high distinction in the war and its record-setting decoration count earned it the nickname "Purple Heart Battalion" and its motto, in keeping with its tenacious fighting spirit, was "Go for Broke."

MAXIM #4

NEVER SHARE A FOXHOLE WITH ANYONE BRAVER THAN YOURSELF & FAMOUS LAST STANDS

Statue of a Sikh soldier at Saragarhi

The Battle of Saragarhi was fought before the Tirah Campaign on 12 September, 1897 between Sikh soldiers of the British Indian Army and Pashtun Orakzai tribesmen. It occurred in the Northwest Frontier Province (now Khyber Pakhtunkhwa, Pakistan).

The British Indian contingent comprised 21 Sikh soldiers of the 36th Sikhs (now the 4th battalion of the Sikh Regiment), who were stationed at an army post and were attacked by around 10,000 Afghans. The Sikhs, led by Havildar Ishar Singh, chose to fight to the death, in what is considered by some military historians as one of history's greatest last stands. The post was recaptured two days later by another British Indian contingent.

All 21 Sikh non-commissioned officers and soldiers of other ranks who laid down their lives in the Battle of Saragarhi were from the Majha region of Punjab and were posthumously awarded the Indian Order of Merit, at that time the highest gallantry award an Indian soldier could receive. The corresponding gallantry award was the Victoria Cross. The award is equivalent to today's Param Vir Chakra awarded by the President of India.

MAXIM #4
LESSON LEARNED

Stand firm; for well you know that hardship and danger are the price of glory, and that sweet is the savour of a life of courage and of deathless renown above the grave. – Alexander the Great (324 BC in India when the Macedonians refused to go on quoted in the Arrian, The Campaign of Alexander, v, c. AD 150, tr. De Selincourt).

It is men who endure toil and dare dangers that achieve glorious deeds, and it is a lovely thing to live with courage and to die leaving behind an everlasting renown. – Alexander the Great (356–323 BC) quoted in Plutarch 46 AD, The Lives of the Noble Grecians and Romans.

Battle scene on Statue of Alexander the Great, Thessaloniki, Greece – Maxim 4 Lesson Learned

MAXIM #5

EVERY COMMAND WHICH CAN BE MISUNDERSTOOD, WILL BE!

Painting of British Admiral & 1st Viscount Horatio Nelson by Lemuel Francis Abbott – (1760–1802)

Turning a blind eye is an idiom describing the ignoring of undesirable information.

The phrase *to turn a blind eye* is attributed to an incident in the life of Admiral Horatio Nelson. Nelson was blinded in one eye early in his Royal Navy career. In 1801, during the Battle of Copenhagen, cautious Admiral Sir Hyde Parker, in overall command of the British forces, sent a signal to Nelson's forces, giving him discretion to withdraw. Naval orders were transmitted via a system of signal flags at that time. When this order was given to the more aggressive Nelson's attention, he lifted his telescope up to his blind eye, said "I really do not see the signal," and his forces continued to press home the attack.

Despite the popular belief that he was disobeying orders, the signal gave Nelson permission to withdraw at his discretion. Even at the time, some of the people on his ship may have believed otherwise as they were unaware of the exact content of the signal.

MAXIM #5

EVERY COMMAND WHICH CAN BE MISUNDERSTOOD WILL BE!

British Man-of-War Battleship

HMS *Somerset* was an 80-gun third rate ship of the line of the Royal Navy, built to the 1719 Establishment at Woolwich and launched on 21 October 1731. She was the second ship to bear the name.

Lord George Rodney, later to triumph at the Battle of the Saintes in 1782, served in HMS *Somerset* in 1739 while preparing for his lieutenant's exams. The ship saw action at the Battle of Toulon in 1744. Toulon was an infamous engagement and consequently no battle honor was awarded. A combined Franco-Spanish fleet that had been blockaded in Toulon for two years finally put to sea, led by Admiral de la Bruyere de Court. The blockading British fleet under Admiral Thomas Mathews was roughly the same size as the Franco-Spanish fleet but fearing that the enemy fleet movement was designed to force him out of position and allow a troop convoy to reach Italy, Mathews ordered his fleet to attack before forming up into line. Admiral Richard Lestock, Mathew's second in command, appears to have deliberately misunderstood his orders, and the resulting battle was indecisive, with the British taking more damage than they inflicted. Mathews was dismissed from the Navy for failing to obey permanent fighting instructions for battle.

Somerset was broken up in 1746.

MAXIM #5

EVERY COMMAND WHICH CAN BE MISUNDERSTOOD WILL BE!

Depicting the Light Brigade at the moment of reaching the Russian guns. Shown are the 11th Hussars and the 17th Lancers. The all-time classic image of the disastrous Charge of the Light Brigade which included the 17th Lancers, who lead the charge. Lord Cardigan is shown on the left, dressed in his 11th Hussars uniform. The Light Brigade were being kept in reserve after the successful charge of the heavy brigade, but the slow advance of the British infantry to take advantage of the heavy brigade's success had given the Russian forces time to take away artillery

*Painting of the Relief of the Light Brigade
by Richard Caton Woodville – (1856–1927)*

pieces from captured redoubts. Lord Raglan, after seeing this, ordered the light brigade to advance rapidly to the front, follow the enemy and try to prevent them carrying away the guns. This message was taken by Captain Nolan to Lord Lucan, the cavalry commander who could only see the main Russian artillery position at the head of a valley. Lord Lucan then rode over to Cardigan and ordered him to attack these guns. So the Light Brigade charged these Russian guns, and not the guns being taken away by Russian forces from the redoubts. The carnage was great; from the 607 men who started the charge, only 198 returned from action. The Light Brigade was made up of the 4th and 13th Light Dragoons, 8th and 11th Hussars and the 17th Lancers. As French Officer General Pierre Bosquet observed – "It is magnificent, but it is not war."

	Went into Action	Returned from Action	Losses
4th Light Dragoons	118	39	79
8th Hussars	104	38	66
11th Hussars	110	25	85
13th Light Dragoons	130	61	69
17th Lancers	145	35	110
Total:	**607**	**198**	**409**

MAXIM #5

EVERY COMMAND WHICH CAN BE MISUNDERSTOOD WILL BE!

General Daniel E. Sickles & his Staff following the Battle of Gettysburg, 1863

Daniel Sickles – Decision at Gettysburg:

Moving north, Sickles' III Corps reached Gettysburg early on July 2, a day after fighting had commenced. Upon arriving, he received orders from Meade to place his corps on the lower section of Cemetery Ridge, with his right joining with Major General Winfield Scott Hancock's II Corp and his left anchored on a rocky hill known as Little Round Top. Moving onto the assigned ground, Sickles was concerned as his men occupied a low part of the ridge which was opposite higher ground to the west. He also failed to secure Little Round Top as he did not believe he had sufficient men. As the morning progressed, Sickles met with Meade and asked the Union commander to come see the terrain to III Corps' front. Meade refused and initially told Sickles to hold his position. He later softened this order to allow Sickles to deploy as he saw fit, but within the limits of the original instructions.

Later scouting the ground to the west, including the Peach Orchard, with Meade's artillery chief, Brigadier General Henry Hunt, Sickles became increasingly eager to push forward. Though Hunt agreed it was a better position, he could not give Sickles permission to advance. Reporting to Meade, Hunt recommended against allowing Sickles to move as insufficient men were available to hold a line from Cemetery Ridge to the Peach Orchard and back to Little Round Top. As the afternoon passed, Sickles' frustration grew and at 3:00 PM he ordered an advance of his own accord. While Brigadier General Andrew Humphrey's division deployed along the Emmitsburg Road, Brigadier General David Birney's angled southeast from the Peach Orchard past Rose's Woods to Devil's Den.

Shortly after occupying this position, III Corps came under attack from Confederate troops led by Lieutenant General James Longstreet. Overextended and with both flanks in the air, Sickles' position was quickly jeopardized. Arriving on the scene, Meade was horrified and confronted Sickles. After being chastised by his superior, Sickles offered to pull back, but the Confederate attacks prevented this from happening. In intense fighting, III Corps was overwhelmed and began retreating as Meade rushed reinforcements to the area. With his salient crumbling, Sickles was struck in the right leg by shrapnel. Falling, his leg was immediately amputated. While the Union line managed to hold, Sickles requested transportation to Washington. Arriving on July 4, he brought news of the Union victory which was secured the day before. Preserving his severed right leg, Sickles donated it to the Army Medical Museum.

MAXIM #5

EVERY COMMAND WHICH CAN BE MISUNDERSTOOD WILL BE!

Spanish Civil War Magazine Cover dated 31 March 1937

George Orwell, the renowned writer and British volunteer who served in the Republican Army during the Spanish Civil War in 1936, reflects upon the tragic-comic misunderstandings that often occur during war.

The difficult passwords which the army was using at this time were a minor source of danger. They were those tiresome double passwords in which one word has to be answered by another. Usually they were an elevating and revolutionary nature, such as *Cultura-progreso*, or *Seremos-invecibles*, and it was often impossible to get illiterate sentries to remember these highfalutin words. One night, I remember, the password was *Cataluna-eroica*, and a moon-faced peasant lad named Jaime Domenech approached me, greatly puzzled, and asked me to explain.

'*Eroica*-what does *eroica* mean?'

I told him that it meant the same as *valiente*. A little while later he was stumbling up the trench in the darkness, and the sentry challenged him:

'*Alto! Cataluna!*'

'*Valiente!*' yelled Jaime, certain that he was saying the right thing.

Bang!

However, the sentry missed him. In this war everyone always did miss everyone else, when it was humanly possible.

MAXIM #5

EVERY COMMAND WHICH CAN BE MISUNDERSTOOD, WILL BE!

Anzac Cove is a small cove on the Gallipoli peninsula in Turkey. It became famous as the site of World War I landing of the ANZACs on 25 April 1915

The **Battle of the Nek** was a small World War I battle fought as part of the Gallipoli campaign. "The Nek" was a narrow stretch of ridge in the Anzac battlefield on the Gallipoli peninsula. The name derives from the Afrikaans word for a "mountain pass" but the terrain itself was a perfect bottleneck and easy to defend, as had been proven during a Turkish attack in May. It connected the Anzac trenches on the ridge known as "Russell's Top" to the knoll called "Baby 700," on which the Turkish defenders were entrenched. In total area, the Nek, according to noted historian Charles Bean, is about a strip of land the size of three tennis courts.

Battle of the Nek Prelude:

For the three months since the Allied landing at Gallipoli on April 25, 1915, the Anzac beachhead had been a stalemate. In August, Allied planners, in an effort to break the deadlock, proposed a new bold offensive to capture the high ground of the Sari Bair range that linked the Anzac front with the new landing to the north of Suvla. In addition to the main advance north out of the Anzac perimeter, several supporting attacks were planned from the existing trench positions.

The attack at the Nek was meant to coincide with an attack by New Zealand troops from Chunuk Bair, which was to be captured during the night. The Australian 3rd Light Horse Brigade, commanded by Colonel F.G. Hughes and consisting of the 8th (Victorian), 9th (Victorian & South Australian) and 10th (Western Australian) Light Horse Regiments, was directed to attack across the Nek to Baby 700 while the New Zealanders descended from the rear onto Battleship Hill, the next knoll above Baby 700.

The general plan first called for the naval bombardment of the enemy positions atop of the Sari Bair range followed by an infantry ground attack launched at 5:30 am by the Australian 3rd Light Horse Brigade who would destroy the entrenched Turkish machine gun positions (the Australian cavalry had left its horses in Egypt in May and was now was tasked to serve as infantry reinforcements).

As far as the tactical plan was concerned, the Australian 8th and 10th Light Horse regiments were to advance on a front 80 meters wide in a total of four waves of 150 men each, two waves per regiment. Each wave would advance two minutes apart. The distance they would have to travel to reach the Turkish line was approximately 27 meters. Colored marker flags were carried, to be shown from the captured trenches to indicate success.

MAXIM #5

EVERY COMMAND WHICH CAN BE MISUNDERSTOOD WILL BE!

Battle of the Nek Prelude continued:

Unfortunately, however, it became quickly apparent that the prerequisites for the attack had not been met. More specifically, there would be no simultaneous attack from the rear of Baby 700. The New Zealand advance was held up and they were not to reach Chunuk Bair until the morning of 8 August, a day late. To further complicate matters, an attack from Steele's Post against German Officers' Trench by the 6th Battalion, 2nd Infantry Brigade of the Australian 1st Division, had also failed. Nevertheless, Major General Sir Alexander Godley, commander of the New Zealand and Australian Division of which the 3rd Light Horse Brigade was then a part, declared that the attack was still to proceed.

Due to a failure to synchronize watches, the attack was launched seven minutes late, giving the Turkish defenders ample time to return to their trenches and prepare for the assault. The first wave of 150 men from the 8th Light Horse Regiment, led by their commander, Lieutenant Colonel A.H. White, went over the top late and ran into a hail of machine gun and rifle fire. A few men reached the Turkish trenches, and marker flags were reportedly seen flying, but they were quickly overwhelmed.

The second wave of 150 followed the first without question and met the same fate. This was the ultimate tragedy of the Nek, that the attack was not halted after the first wave when it was abundantly clear that it was futile. A simultaneous attack by the 2nd Light Horse Regiment (1st Light Horse Brigade) at Quinn's Post against the Turkish trench system known as "The Chessboard" was abandoned after 49 out of the 50 men in the first wave became casualties. In this case, the regiment's commander had not deployed with the first wave and so was able to make the decision to abort.

Lieutenant Colonel N.M. Brazier, commander of the 10th Light Horse Regiment, attempted to have the third wave canceled, claiming that "the whole thing was nothing but bloody murder." He was unable to find Colonel Hughes and unable to persuade the brigade major, Colonel J.M. Antill, who believed the reports that marker flags had been sighted. So the third wave attacked and was wiped out. Finally, Hughes called off the attack, but confusion in the fire trench led to some of the fourth wave going over.

Canakkale Martyrs Memorial in Gallipoli, Turkey

MAXIM #5

EVERY COMMAND WHICH CAN BE MISUNDERSTOOD WILL BE!

Photo of The Nek Cemetery, Anzac, Gallipoli

Battle of the Nek Aftermath:

A further consequence of the failure to call off the attack at the Nek was that a supporting attack by two companies of the Royal Welch Fusiliers was launched from the head of Monash Valley, between Russell's Top and Pope's Hill, against the "Chessboard" trenches. Before the attack was cancelled, 65 casualties were incurred.

    The Australian casualties from the 3rd Light Horse Brigade numbered 372; 234 from the 8th Light Horse Regiment, of which 154 were killed, and 138 from the 10th, of which 80 were killed. The Turkish losses were negligible on this occasion. When Commonwealth burial parties returned to the peninsula in 1919, the bones of the dead light horsemen were still lying thickly on the small piece of ground.

The Nek Cemetery now covers most of the no-man's land of the tiny battlefield and contains the remains of 316 people, of whom only five could be identified. Trooper Harold Rush of the 10th Light Horse Regiment died in the third wave. His body was one of the few identified and he is buried in Walker's Ridge Cemetery. His epitaph famously reads: *Goodbye Cobber, God Bless You.*

Charles Bean felt this charge would go down as one of the bravest acts in the history of Australians at war. In memorable words, Bean described the scene:

The Nek could be seen crowded with their bodies. At first here and there a man raised his arm to the sky or tried to drink from his water bottle. But as the sun climbed higher … such movement ceased. Over the whole summit the figures lay still in the quivering sun.

MAXIM #5

LESSON LEARNED

No Operational Plan ever survives initial contact. When developing battle plans, adopt the **KISS rule (Keep it Simple Stupid)** to ensure for flexibility and that everyone in the chain of command understands the commander's intent.

General Eisenhower frequently stated that in war, plans are everything before the battle begins, but once the shooting starts, plans are worthless. When Ike graduated first in his class at the Command and General Staff College at Ft. Leavenworth, Patton had written to congratulate him and then warn him to put all that Leavenworth stuff out of his mind from now on. "Victory in the next war," Patton declared, "will depend on Execution Not Plans."

WWI British Staff Officers engaged in Planning – Maxim 5 Lesson Learned

MAXIM #6

NEVER FORGET THAT YOUR WEAPON WAS MADE BY THE LOWEST BIDDER! (WEAPONS THAT "MISSED THE MARK")

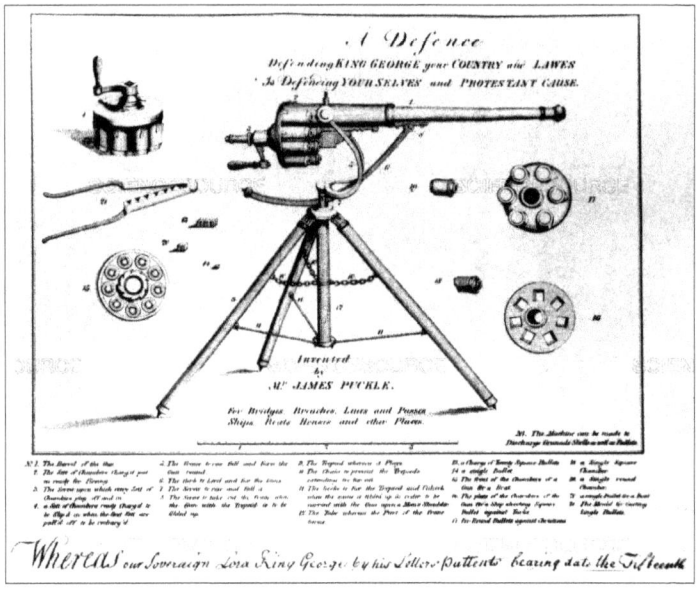

Illustration of Puckle's Gun Patent – May 15, 1718

In 1718, James Puckle patented the world's first rapid-fire weapon: The Defense Gun, also known as the Puckle Gun. Resembling a giant revolver on a tripod, this gun claimed to be able to fire 63 shots in seven minutes, which was a rather noteworthy improvement when one considers that the most skilled musketeers at the time could only fire three shots per minute.

The official reason why the Puckle Gun never caught on with the British army was that the weapon was designed with interchangeable cylinders. More specifically, one type of cylinder shot regular round musket balls intended for "civilized people" on the

European continent, while the other interchangeable cylinder shot square bullets intended for Muslim Turks, with the rationale that the square bullets would hurt more. Critics of the gun questioned the efficacy of using square bullets since the square bullets and cylinders posed a problem in manufacturing and, thus, could not be mass produced, not to mention that the weapon's racist orientation offended politically correct, Christian-minded citizens.

MAXIM #6

NEVER FORGET THAT YOUR WEAPON WAS MADE BY THE LOWEST BIDDER! (WEAPONS THAT "MISSED THE MARK")

Photo of the Netopyr Tank – 1914

The **Tsar Tank**, also known as the **Netopyr**, which stands for pipistrellus (a genus of bat) or **Lebedenko Tank,** was an unusual Russian armored vehicle developed by Nikolai Lebedenko, Nikolai Zhukovsky, Boris Stechkin, and Alexander Mikulin from 1914 onwards. The project was scrapped after initial tests deemed the vehicle to be underpowered and vulnerable to artillery fire.

It differed from modern tanks in that it did not use caterpillar tracks—rather, it used a tricycle design. The two front spoked wheels were nearly 27 feet in diameter; the back wheel was smaller, only 5 feet high, triple wheel, to ensure maneuverability. The upper cannon turret reached nearly 24 feet high. The hull was 36 feet wide with two more cannons placed on it. Additional weapons were also planned under the belly. Each wheel was powered by a 250 hp Sunbeam engine.

The vehicle received its nickname because its model, when carried by the back wheel, resembled a bat hanging asleep.

The huge wheels were intended to cross significant obstacles. However, due to miscalculations of the weight, the back wheel was prone to be stuck in soft ground and ditches, and the front wheels were sometimes insufficient to pull it out. This led to a fiasco of tests before the high commission in August 1915. The tank remained in the location where it was tested, some 60 kilometers from Moscow until 1923, when it was finally taken apart for scrap.

MAXIM #6

NEVER FORGET THAT YOUR WEAPON WAS MADE BY THE LOWEST BIDDER! (WEAPONS THAT "MISSED THE MARK")

WWI Photo of a French solider equipped with a Chauchat machine rifle

The **Chauchat**, named after its main contributor Colonel Louis Chauchat, was the standard machine rifle or light machine gun of the French army during World War I (1914–18). Beginning in 1916, it was placed into regular service with French infantry, where the troops called it the **FM Chauchat**.

Between December 1915 and November 1918 262,000 Chauchat machine rifles were manufactured, including 244,000 in the 8 mm Lebel service cartridge, making it the most widely-manufactured automatic weapon of World War I.

The Chauchat machine rifle was one of the first light, fully automatic rifle caliber weapons designed to be carried and fired by a single operator and an assistant, without a heavy tripod or a team of gunners. It set a precedent for several subsequent 20th century firearm projects, being a portable yet full-power automatic weapon built inexpensively and in very large numbers. The Chauchat combined a pistol grip, an in-line stock, a detachable magazine, and a selective fire capability in a compact package of manageable weight (20 pounds) for a single soldier. Furthermore, it could be fired from the hip and while walking (marching fire).

Despite the advantages of a highly portable automatic weapon that increased the firepower of infantry squads while they progressed forward during their assaults, the muddy trenches of northern France exposed a number of flaws in the Chauchat's design. Construction had been simplified to facilitate mass production, resulting in low quality of many metal parts. The magazines in particular were the cause of about 75% of the stoppages or cessations of fire. They were made of thin stamped metal and open on one side, allowing easy ingress of mud and dust. The weapon also ceased to function when overheated, the barrel sleeve remaining in the retracted position until the gun had cooled off. Closed-sided magazines were evaluated but never placed into actual service. The A.E.F. in France eventually replaced the Chauchat, at least partially, with the Browning Automatic Rifle, which appeared on the front lines of northern France in September 1918, only two months before the Armistice of November 11. After World War I, the French army replaced the Chauchat as the standard light machine gun with the more effective and gas-operated Mle 1924 light machine gun. In light of all of these weapons malfunctions, several modern experts assessed it as the "worst machine gun" ever fielded in military history.

MAXIM #6

NEVER FORGET THAT YOUR WEAPON WAS MADE BY THE LOWEST BIDDER! (WEAPONS THAT "MISSED THE MARK")

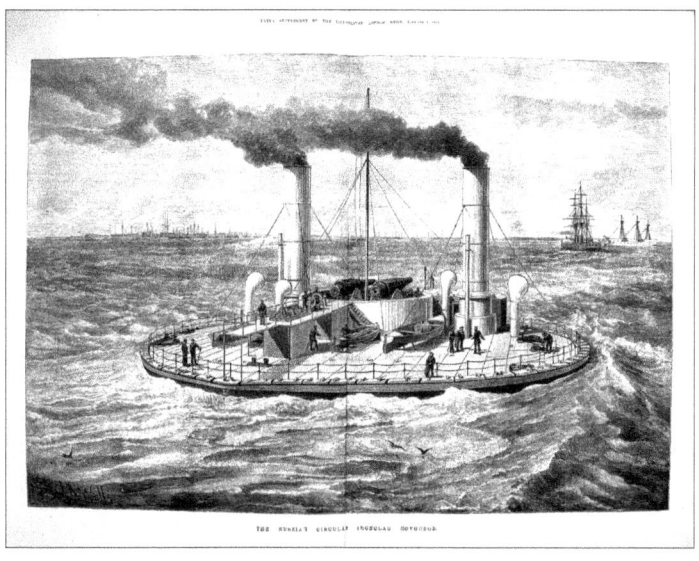

Illustration of the Russian Novgorod Battleship

The ***Novgorod*** was an Imperial Russian warship. It was one of the most unusual warships ever constructed, and still survives in popular naval myth, often described as the "ugliest warship ever built." Together with her near-sister ship Rear Admiral Popov, they were affectionately called "popovkas." after their chief designer. The hull was circular (viewed from the top) intended to be a particularly stable platform for guns but proving to be almost un-maneuverable in practice. She was designed by Andrei Alexandrovich Popov of the Imperial Russian Navy with the purpose of creating a stable platform armed with a few heavy guns that could operate in coastal waters and be well protected by armor plating.

The perceived advantage of the circular hull form was that a shallow-draught vessel could be built with a greater displacement; a small ship could then carry the same armament as a much larger vessel with a more typical hull form. For comparison, a 100-foot-long (30 m) by 13-foot beam (4.0 m) and 13-foot draught vessel would only displace about 2,500 tons.

The primary armament of **Novgorod** was two 26-ton 11-inch guns mounted on separate revolving turntables that could be moved independently or together. Recoil was suppressed by a hydraulic frictional compressor, and by wedges placed in the after-part of their platforms.

The ship was driven by six engines, each with their own propeller shaft. Boiler and engine rooms occupied fully half of the interior hull space. The boilers were placed in two separate compartments, one on either beam. Four steam launches were usually carried on deck.

In practice, the **Novgorod** and her near-sister **Rear Admiral Popov** was a disaster, a fact that became abundantly clear as it floated into the Danube to take part in the Russo-Turkish War of 1877–1878. They pitched and rolled excessively, even in moderate seas. They were slow, poorly maneuverable, and vulnerable to plunging fire. Worst, though, was that the off-axis recoil of the guns would impart a centrifugal rotation to the ship. In operational use, these ships would have to throw their single rudder hard over during firing to act as "water brakes." This severely restricted the aiming and rate-of-fire of the main guns.

After enduring much snickering from the Turks, the Russians re-designated them as "Coastal Defense Armor-Clad Ships" in 1892, and then relegated them to be tied up at port as store ships in 1903. They were finally relegated to the scrapyard in 1912.

MAXIM #6

NEVER FORGET THAT YOUR WEAPON WAS MADE BY THE LOWEST BIDDER! (WEAPONS THAT "MISSED THE MARK")

Photo of the German V-3, WWII

The V-3 *Hochdruckpumpe* (aka HDP, '*Fleissiges Lieschen*'; '*Tausend Fussler*' or 'London gun') was a supergun designed by Saar Roechling during World War II. The 140-meter long cannon was capable of delivering a 140 kg shell over a 165 km range. In effect, if fired from the coast of France, the lobbed shell could easily reach London.

In, September 1943 at Mimoyecques, France, hundreds of slave workers began construction of a 30-meter deep bunker that would house the gun. Upon discovering the German plan, the French Resistance informed the Allies, which led to the site being bombed two months later. Initially the bunker proved impervious to Allied bombs. However, through persistent efforts, when the weapon was nearing completion, on July 6, 1944, the Royal Air Force 617 squadron (also known as The Dam Busters) ultimately proved successful by dropping three 5400-kilogram

Tallboy bombs through the gun shaft openings. The bombs penetrated 30 meters to the first level of the complex and exploded, killing approximately 300 workers. By the end of August, the Germans completely abandoned the complex in the face of the advancing British forces.

WWII Photo of the Experimental German Vortex "Windkanone" (Wind Cannon) on the gun park at the German artillery testing range at Hillersleben, May 1945

During World War II, Hitler's Third Reich was continually devising ingenious, unconventional methods to shoot down Allied planes. One illustration of this is Hitler's famous "Air Rifle" or Vortex Cannon, which was manufactured in a factory near Stuttgart. The weapon is best described as being a massive air cannon with a 3-foot diameter and 35-foot-long cast-iron tube that was packed with an explosive mixture of hydrogen and ammonia and that, upon detonation, would eject a "shell" of compressed air. The Nazis hoped these shells would create whirlwinds to swat Allied planes out of the sky.

In trials, the *WindKanone* was a destructive force. The weapon shattered wooden planks from 650 feet away. Still, there's a big difference between breaking stationary lumber and nailing airborne targets. Even when the gusts nailed planes flying as low as 500 feet, pilots were barely thrown off course. Never ones to waste creative energy, the Nazis redeployed the air cannon as an anti-infantry weapon. But it was hopeless in the field as well—its gargantuan size made it an easy target for bombs. After a few disastrous outings, the WindKanone sat unused, gathering rust at a testing facility until confused American troops stumbled across it in April 1945.

MAXIM #6

NEVER FORGET THAT YOUR WEAPON WAS MADE BY THE LOWEST BIDDER!
(WEAPONS THAT "MISSED THE MARK")

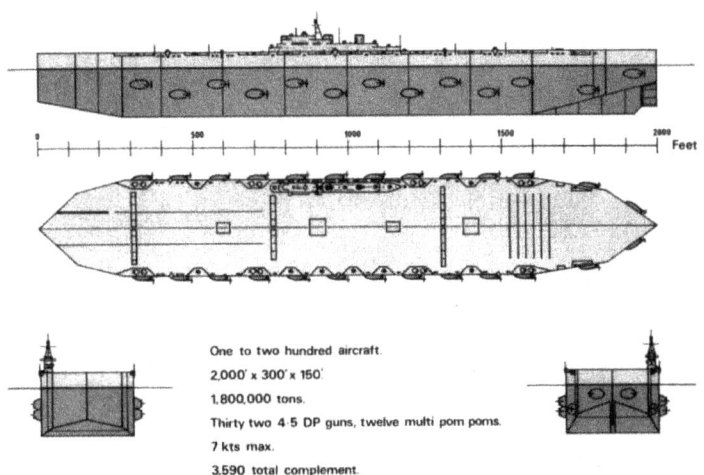

Illustration of the British HMS Habbakuk Pykrete Warship from 1932 Article —Ice Island of Dr. Gerke

During World War II, aircraft carriers were in short supply. So were steel and aluminum, the main materials needed to build the gargantuan ships. As the Allies scrounged to build vessels, they were also hunting for fresh ideas. So when Geoffrey Pyke, a plucky British inventor, proposed a scheme to build carriers out of ice, the British government jumped on board.

Pyke's concept was to construct the vessels using pykrete—a stronger-than-ice mixture of 86 percent water and 14 percent wood pulp. But it wasn't until construction began on a 1,000-ton model in Canada that engineers encountered the problem of "plastic flow." In layman's terms, the ship started to melt, which caused it to sag under its own weight unless kept at a crisp 3°F. The designers attempted to sidestep the issue by rigging the boat with a complex refrigeration system and reinforcements consisting of 10,000 tons of steel—the very resource they'd been trying to avoid using in the first place.

MAXIM #6

NEVER FORGET THAT YOUR WEAPON WAS MADE BY THE LOWEST BIDDER! (WEAPONS THAT "MISSED THE MARK")

Kalinin K-7 was a real Russian bomber designed in 1933 by WW-I aviator Konstatin Kalinin.

According to *The World's Worst Aircraft – From Pioneering Failures to Multimillion Dollar Disasters* by Jim Winchester, the plane had a wingspan greater than the American B-52.

The bomber was 91 feet long and had seven 750HP engines, 6 on the leading edge of the wing and one at the rear of the fuselage. The K-7 had a wingspan of nearly 174 feet and could fly

Photo of The Kalinin K-7

at a maximum speed of 145 miles per hour. The aircraft was also designed for other functions such as transporting VIP, paratrooper and heavy cargo such as tanks. According to the Kharkov State Aircraft Manufacturing Company (KSAMC) in the Ukraine, the K-7 actually first took to the skies on August 19, 1933 and her final flight was on November 23rd of that year. Winchester's book noted that the prototype was plagued by vibrations and instability problems caused by the massive propeller engines.

Kalinin and his team of engineers tried to overcome flaws by reducing the size of the tail boom. The eleventh test flight proved to be fatal when the plane's elevator jammed, causing it to plow into the ground below. The entire crew of 15 perished.

The Soviet government under the command of Joseph Stalin terminated the project and in 1938 arrested and executed Kalinin for espionage and sabotage.

MAXIM #6

NEVER FORGET THAT YOUR WEAPON WAS MADE BY THE LOWEST BIDDER! (WEAPONS THAT "MISSED THE MARK")

Hitler's Blitzkrieg attack strategy relied on employing dense concentrations of armored, motorized and mechanized formations reinforced by close air support to break through the enemy's defense and defeat them in swift and decisive fashion. However, despite the awesome destructive power of the Panzers, the German army discovered that their forward progress was impeded by several rivers as well as enemy units deployed at the other end of the bridges.

The Nazis, being consummate pragmatists & battlefield innovators, sought to solve the problem of fording rivers in expedient fashion with several hundred feet of rubber tubing and, thus, the Snorkel Tank was born.

Photo of a WWII German Snorkel Tank

In short order, 168 Tauchpanzer II tanks were sealed water-tight and equipped with giant rubber snorkels that were mounted to their hatches. The idea was that the tanks would arrive at a river bank, then drive on the bottom of the river, using the rubber hose as a snorkel for air. Then the tank would appear on the other river bank and surprise the enemy.

Why it failed:

Believe it or not, the tanks proved to be buoyant despite weighing over 25 tons. In effect, the tanks had just enough air in them that they floated a few inches off of the bottom of the rivers. Unfortunately, however, most of the tank commanders quickly discovered that they did not have any traction to navigate to the opposing river bank and then noticed that their vehicles were rapidly filling with water and many drowned in place. For those who managed to exit through the hatches and swim to the surface, many found themselves to be lucrative targets of opportunity with enemy sharpshooters.

MAXIM #6

NEVER FORGET THAT YOUR WEAPON WAS MADE BY THE LOWEST BIDDER! (WEAPONS THAT "MISSED THE MARK")

With the shortage of anti-tank weapons during World War II, the British army developed the Anti-Tank Hand Grenade #74, commonly known as "the sticky grenade." The term "sticky" is appropriate in that a powerful adhesive was applied to an encased metal ball grenade with a 5 second fuse that would come

The "Sticky" Grenade or "Satan's Maraca"

apart after removing the pin. In effect, once a soldier identified an enemy tank, he would sneak up on it and stick the grenade directly to it, release the handle and run away as fast as he could before the grenade exploded.

British Home Guard member Bill Miles recalls: *"It was while practicing that a Home Guard bomber got his sticky bomb stuck to his trouser leg and couldn't shift it. A quick-thinking mate whipped the trousers off and got rid of them and the bomb. After the following explosion, the trousers were in a bit of a mess —- though I think they were a bit of a mess prior to the explosion."* In other words, he crapped all over himself.

Although the sticky grenade was originally rejected for use by the British army, Winston Churchill nevertheless ordered them to be manufactured and furnished to both the Home Guard and the French Resistance. They also were used in limited fashion by British 8th Army soldiers in North Africa, where they claimed a grand total of six German tanks as well as an undisclosed number of British trousers.

MAXIM #6

NEVER FORGET THAT YOUR WEAPON WAS MADE BY THE LOWEST BIDDER! (WEAPONS THAT "MISSED THE MARK")

Photo of the Scooter with 75 mm Mounted Cannon

Used by the French during Vietnam, this vehicle was put together when the French military was lacking the money to provide more sophisticated equipment. They used what they had and often had to improvise in order to try to keep the military equipped. The Scooter-Mounted Cannon vehicle held a 75mm cannon. It was mainly used by paratroopers during the 1950s. However, it's safe to say that this didn't last long, as it surely offered no type of protection or even stability during war.

MAXIM #6

NEVER FORGET THAT YOUR WEAPON WAS MADE BY THE LOWEST BIDDER! (WEAPONS THAT "MISSED THE MARK")

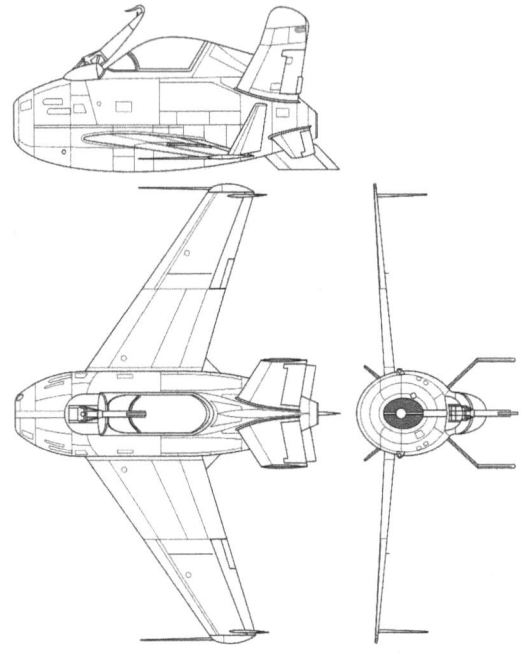

Illustration of the McDonnell XF-85 Goblin

The **McDonnell XF-85 Goblin** was an American prototype fighter aircraft conceived during World War II by McDonnell Aircraft. It was intended to be deployed from the bomb bay of the giant Convair B-36 bomber as a parasite fighter. The XF-85's intended role was to defend bombers from hostile interceptors, a need demonstrated during World War II.

The first time test pilot Ed Schoch attempted to get the plane back into the belly, the trapeze hook they were trying to snag him with smashed through his canopy, knocking him unconscious and tearing away his flight helmet. Luckily, he woke up before an unscheduled air/ground interface, at which point he managed to land the crippled aircraft on skids, a dangerous maneuver made necessary by the fact that the Goblin was designed without landing gear. Not surprising, four out of the six test flights ended up with similar crash landings in the desert, which presumably explains why Ed Schoch was the only pilot that flew all six missions.

Despite the cancellation of the XF-85, the USAF continued to examine the concept of parasite aircraft as defensive fighters through a series of projects including Project MX-106 "Tip Tow," Project FICON, and Project "Tom-Tom" which involved fighter aircraft attached to bomber aircraft by their wingtips. Project FICON ("fighter conveyor") emerged as an effective Convair GRB-36D and Republic RF-84K Thunderflash combined bomber-reconnaissance-fighter, although the role was changed to that of strategic reconnaissance. Project FICON drew heavily on data from the abortive XF-85 project and closely followed McDonnell's recommendations in designing a more refined trapeze. A total of 10 converted B-36s and 25 reconnaissance fighters saw limited service with the Strategic Air Command in 1955–1956 before being supplemented by more effective aircraft and satellite systems.

MAXIM #6

NEVER FORGET THAT YOUR WEAPON WAS MADE BY THE LOWEST BIDDER! (WEAPONS THAT "MISSED THE MARK")

U.S. Navy photo of specially-trained bottlenose dolphin wearing a pinger device on his fin leaping out of the water while training March 18, 2003 in the Arabian Gulf

During the Cold War, both the USSR and USA outfitted dolphins with weapons to carry out a myriad of missions, to include laying underwater mines, kamikaze attacking submarines, and fighting enemy dolphins. Despite some initial successes, the program was ultimately shelved because several dolphins were unable to distinguish friendly forces from enemy targets.

U.S. Air Force photo of C123 performing aerial spray mission – Operation Ranch Hand, Vietnam War

After the banning of mustard gas on the battlefield, American scientists worked to create a non-lethal gas that could stun enemy combatants. Their eventual solution, Calming Gas, was an extremely concentrated form of plant smoke that could be released from an airplane. This gas was taken out of use when it was discovered that American troops were using it on themselves, causing them to ravenously consume rations and to giggle while in combat.

MAXIM #6

NEVER FORGET THAT YOUR WEAPON WAS MADE BY THE LOWEST BIDDER! (WEAPONS THAT "MISSED THE MARK")

Photo of Solid-State Active Denial Weapon System – U.S. Army

In 2010, the U.S. military deployed a weapon in Afghanistan known as the Active Denial System which was comprised of a satellite dish size device that was designed to emit an extremely high frequency wave that would paralyze the Taliban. However, after spending over $40 million and over a decade of research, the military recalled the weapon after about a month because the weapon failed to deliver a debilitating blast. Rather, the ray merely caused enemy insurgents to suffer a mild sunburn.

MAXIM #6

NEVER FORGET THAT YOUR WEAPON WAS MADE BY THE LOWEST BIDDER! (WEAPONS THAT "MISSED THE MARK")

Photo of Scalable Compact Ultra-Short Pulse Laser System- U.S. Army

Many weapons have the unfortunate side effect of being lethal, so defense agencies are always on the lookout for more humane ways to stun the enemy into submission. In 2007, the military spent $800,000 to develop the "sick stick" gadget: a cumbersome 15" long x 4' wide flashlight that unleashed a kaleidoscopic pulse that caused vertigo, nausea, and hurling.

The idea for the weapon originated during the 1950s, when helicopter pilots began mysteriously crashing. Investigators determined that the frequency of choppy flashes of sunlight shining through a chopper's spinning blades caused dizziness and disorientation. Tinted glass and helmet visors solved the pilots' problems, but the U.S. military started wondering whether it could use this particular effect to its advantage. Despite the creative idea, the weapon suffered serious flaws. First, it required that the target look directly at the light in order to feel the effects. Further, once the target discovered that the nauseating effects were caused by the beam of light, he would either simply turn and run or wear sunglasses to mitigate the effects. Needless to say, both the Department of Homeland Security and military abandoned the project.

The U.S. army is now working on a nonlethal weapon known as SCUPLS (Scalable Ultra-Short Pulse Laser) that is somewhat akin to the Star Trek's fictional phaser. This weapon will have the ability to warn, dazzle, deafen, stun or burn depending on what settings are used.

MAXIM #6

NEVER FORGET THAT YOUR WEAPON WAS MADE BY THE LOWEST BIDDER! (WEAPONS THAT "MISSED THE MARK")

During the 1970s and 1980s, rumors swirled that the Soviets had developed a chemical substance that could be used to make nuclear bombs as small as watermelons. Known as "red mercury,"

the substance reportedly fetched up to $1 million for a single kilogram, and the alleged super weapon set off a frenzy of speculation over whether it might land in terrorists' hands.

Red Mercury was a chemical substance developed by the USSR as a fission material that could be used to create extremely precise nuclear reactions. A number of Red Mercury guns were confiscated from KGB agents who tried to enter Canada in the 1980s. Canadian scientists took apart the guns and discovered Red Mercury made both a great toothpaste and a cure to erectile dysfunction, but not a magic fission material, after all.

MAXIM #6

NEVER FORGET THAT YOUR WEAPON WAS MADE BY THE LOWEST BIDDER! (WEAPONS THAT "MISSED THE MARK")

Space Cannon

Short of the Death Star, the Russian Elipton Cannon is the most powerful laser weapon in space. It's capable of wiping out an entire city with just one blast. At least it will be when its batteries recharge from its successful test firing. Russian scientists estimate that it will have collected enough solar energy to fire again by 2316.

MAXIM #6

LESSON LEARNED

The Pentagon now spends about $21.6 million every hour to procure new military systems. As the cost and complexity of defense acquisitions programs continue to spiral out of control, many defense experts believe runaway military spending is unsustainable. Meanwhile, soldiers in the field are being denied much-needed equipment. Escalating complexity, a shortage of trained workers, and crass politicization mean that most programs to develop new military systems fail to meet expectations.

Always be wary of new weapon systems and ensure that you have an adequate supply of parts if things start breaking down.

Photo of a catastrophic weapons failure

Disassembled M-16 A-1 Rifle – U.S. Army Operator's Manual for M16, M16A1 Rifle & Field Manual – FM 3–22.9

MAXIM #7

NO OPLAN EVER SURVIVES INITIAL CONTACT; i.e. THERE IS NO SUCH THING AS A PERFECT PLAN

Photo of General P.T. Beauregard–1862

Pierre Gustave Toutant-Beauregard (May 28, 1818–February 20, 1893) became the first Brigadier General in the Confederate States Army. He commanded the defenses of Charleston, South Carolina at the start of the Civil War at Fort Sumter on April 12, 1861. Three months later he won the First Battle of Bull Run near Manassas, Virginia.

Beauregard commanded armies in the Western Theater, including at the Battle of Shiloh in Tennessee and the Siege of Corinth in northern Mississippi. He returned to Charleston and defended it in 1863 from repeated naval and land attacks by Union forces. His greatest achievement was saving the important industrial city of Petersburg, Virginia, in June 1864, and thus the nearby Confederate capital of Richmond, from assaults by overwhelmingly superior Union Army forces.

His influence over Confederate strategy was lessened by his poor professional relationships with President Jefferson Davis and other senior generals and officials.

President Davis considered many of Beauregard's plans to be impractical for an inexperienced army. Throughout the war, Davis and Beauregard would argue about Beauregard's tendencies to devise grand strategies based on formal Napoleonic military principles. In effect, Davis claimed that he lacked a pragmatic understanding of logistics and intelligence and was ineffectual in weighing the relative military strengths.

MAXIM #7

NO OPLAN EVER SURVIVES INITIAL CONTACT; i.e. THERE IS NO SUCH THING AS A PERFECT PLAN

The **Bay of Pigs Invasion** (Spanish: **Invasión de Playa Girón** or **Invasión de Bahía de Cochinos** or **Batalla de Girón**) was a failed military invasion of Cuba undertaken by the CIA-sponsored paramilitary group Brigade 2506 on 17 April 1961. A counter-revolutionary military, trained and funded by the United States government's Central Intelligence Agency (CIA), Brigade 2506 fronted the armed wing of the Democratic Revolutionary Front (DRF) and intended to overthrow the increasingly communist government of Fidel Castro. Launched from Guatemala, the invading force was defeated within three days by the Cuban Revolutionary Armed Forces, under the direct command of Prime Minister Fidel Castro.

The Cuban Revolution of 1952 to 1959 had forced dictator Fulgencio Batista, an ally of the United States, into exile. He was replaced by the 26th July Movement led by Castro, which severed the country's formerly strong links with the US after expropriating American economic assets and developing links with the Soviet Union, with whom, at the time, the United States was engaged in the Cold War. US President Dwight D. Eisenhower was concerned at the direction Castro's government was taking, and in March 1960 he allocated $13.1 million to the CIA to plan Castro's overthrow. The CIA proceeded to organize the operation with the aid of various Cuban counter-revolutionary forces, training Brigade 2506 in Guatemala. Eisenhower's successor John F. Kennedy approved the final invasion plan on 4 April 1961.

Over 1,400 paramilitaries, divided into five infantry battalions and one paratrooper battalion, assembled in Guatemala before setting out for Cuba by boat on 13 April 1961. Two days later on 15 April, eight CIA-supplied B-26 bombers attacked Cuban airfields and then returned to the US. On the night of 16 April, the main invasion landed at a beach named Playa Girón in the Bay of Pigs. It initially overwhelmed a local revolutionary militia. The Cuban army's counter-offensive was led by José Ramón Fernández before Castro decided to take personal control of the operation. As the US involvement became apparent to the world, Kennedy decided against providing further air cover for the invasion. On 20

April, the invaders surrendered, with the majority of troops being publicly interrogated and put into Cuban prisons.

The failed invasion strengthened the position of Castro's leadership as well as his ties with the Soviet Union. This led eventually to the events of the Cuban Missile Crisis of 1962. The invasion was a major embarrassment for US foreign policy; US President John F. Kennedy ordered a number of internal investigations across Latin America.

MAXIM #7
LESSON LEARNED

"No plan of operation extends with any certainty beyond the first contact with the main hostile force. Only the layman thinks that he can see in the course of the campaign the consequent execution of the original idea with all the details thought out in advance and adhered to until the very end." –-Helmuth von Moltke, chief of the Prussian general staff during the wars of German unification. Or, as someone else said, "A plan does not survive the first bullet that flies."

"A good plan violently executed now is better than a perfect plan executed next week." – George S. Patton.

Prior Planning Prevents "Piss" Poor Performance

MAXIM #8

PROFESSIONAL SOLDIERS ARE PREDICTABLE; THE WORLD IS FULL OF DANGEROUS AMATEURS

December 21, 1866 around 12 noon. Captain William Fetterman and the remnants of his 81-man patrol fight to the last man on Infantry Hill against over 1,000 Lakota warriors led by Crazy Horse. The entire battle only lasted about 30 minutes.

In November 1866, a brash Civil War veteran named Captain William Fetterman arrives at Fort Phil Kearney, Wyoming to serve with the 18th U.S. Infantry.

He soon discovers that Fort Phil Kearney is right in the middle of Red Cloud's War. Though the mission of the fort is to secure the Bozeman Trail for civilian traffic, it hasn't gone well. In fact, civilian commerce trickled to a halt on the two-year-old trail by the end of that previous summer. Led by Chief Red Cloud and Crazy Horse, the Indians are conducting a textbook guerrilla war. Rather than stage large attacks on the fortified post, their hit-and-run attacks and ambushes make life difficult and dangerous for anyone outside of it.

The commander of the post, Colonel Henry Carrington, is a cautious man whose greatest fear is a mass attack on the fort, which he expects is imminent. Already short of men, horses and ammo and equipped mostly with muzzle loading rifles from the Civil War, Carrington keeps his troops and officers on a short leash – just in case. As a result, Red Cloud has complete freedom of movement. He chooses when, where and how to fight, putting Carrington completely in the reactive mode.

This has many of the garrison officers grumbling about the tactics, since they believe they should be aggressively seeking out the enemy instead of riding shotgun on logging wagons and getting picked off one or two at a time. Since arriving in July, the troopers have already fought over 50 skirmishes and have lost over 150 men with little if anything to show for it.

Fetterman, despite having no experience fighting the Indians, openly expresses his contempt for the Indians' fighting ability and Carrington's cautious tactics and ultimately marches into Colonel Carrington's office on December 21, 1866 to demand an assignment to engage Red Cloud's Sioux warriors. He famously states, "Give me 80 men and I'll ride through the whole Sioux Nation." Carrington obliges the young fire-brand's request and bids him "God's Speed."

Days later, when the patrol failed to return to the Fort, Carrington dispatches another patrol to ascertain their whereabouts. They later discover that Fetterman and his 80 troopers were stripped of their clothes and horribly mutilated.

MAXIM #8

PROFESSIONAL SOLDIERS ARE PREDICTABLE; THE WORLD IS FULL OF DANGEROUS AMATEURS

Adolph Hitler with Generals Keitel & Halder and staff at Brauchitsch's headquarters 1941

Hitler declares war on the United States, 1941. Most historians rate *Operation Barbarossa*, Hitler's attack on the Soviet Union, to have been his worst military blunder of the entire war. However, others may assert that Hitler's almost casual declaration of war against the United States on December 11, 1941 proved to be even more decisively disastrous.

It wasn't necessary. Four days after Pearl Harbor, the US had made no moves against Hitler. Consider the state of the war from the German point of view: it clearly made sense to keep America out of the conflict. Despite the huge support ("all short of war") that the US had been providing Britain since 1940, the U-Boat campaign was going extremely well. By 1941, sinkings had reached a peak, at which rate Britain would have lost fully one-fourth of her merchant fleet within the coming year. In the US, the "America First" movement still had considerable support. A Gallup Poll of October 22, 1941 reported that only 17% of Americans actually favored war with Germany, and as late as the summer of 1942, polls showed that nearly one-third favored a compromise peace with Germany. "I can see why we're fighting the Japs," commented one respondent, "but I can't see why we're fighting the Krauts."

After Pearl Harbor, it was only natural that the powerful "Pacific First" lobby, headed by the redoubtable Admiral Ernest J. King, then CinC US Atlantic Fleet and subsequently Chief of Naval Operations, would urge Roosevelt to attack Japan, then Germany.

If Admiral King and the "Pacific Firsters" had had their way, Britain and an almost mortally wounded Russia would have been left to fight Hitler alone. Had Russia been smashed in 1942, as was all too likely, a subsequent Anglo-American victory in Europe using conventional weapons would have been inconceivable.

Why, then, did Hitler take this fateful decision? Like Saddam Hussein half a century later, he fell prey to his own propaganda, accepting poor intelligence, coupled with his own parochial ignorance, into grossly underestimating US military potential. Secondly, he was convinced that the war in Russia was as good as won. Information available in Moscow since *glasnost* now confirms that as of December 1941, Hitler had good reason to judge Stalin to be in the market for a separate peace.

His miscalculation was the West's salvation.

MAXIM #8

PROFESSIONAL SOLDIERS ARE PREDICTABLE; THE WORLD IS FULL OF DANGEROUS AMATEURS

As far as Saddam Hussein being a great military strategist, he is neither a strategist, nor is he schooled in the operational arts, nor is he a tactician, nor is he a general, nor is he a soldier. Other than that, he's a great military man, I want you to know that. – US Army GENERAL Norman Schwarzkopf

Saddam Hussein – President of Iraq

The **Gulf War** (2 August 1990–28 February 1991), codenamed **Operation Desert Shield** (2 August 1990–17 January 1991), for operations leading to the buildup of troops and defense of Saudi Arabia and **Operation Desert Storm** (17 January 1991–28 February 1991) in its combat phase, was a war waged by coalition forces from 34 nations led by the United States against Iraq in response to Iraq's invasion and annexation of Kuwait.

The initial conflict to expel Iraqi troops from Kuwait began with an aerial and naval bombardment on 17 January 1991, continuing for five weeks. This was followed by a ground assault on 24 February. This was a decisive victory for the Coalition forces, who liberated Kuwait and advanced into Iraqi territory. The Coalition ceased its advance and declared a cease-fire 100 hours after the ground campaign started. Aerial and ground combat was confined to Iraq, Kuwait, and areas on Saudi Arabia's border. Iraq launched Scud missiles against Coalition military targets in Saudi Arabia and against Israel. Though the Persian Gulf War was initially considered an unqualified success for the international coalition, simmering conflict in the troubled region led to a second Gulf War– known as the Iraq War, codenamed **Operation Iraqi Freedom**– that began in 2003 and ultimately resulted in the defeat of Iraqi forces and the execution of Saddam Hussein on 30 December 2006.

Iraqi Casualties for Operation Desert Storm

The exact number of Iraqi combat casualties is unknown but is believed to have been heavy. Some estimate that Iraq sustained between 20,000 and 35,000 fatalities. A report commissioned by the U.S. Air Force estimated 10,000–12,000 Iraqi combat deaths in the air campaign, and as many as 10,000 casualties in the ground war. This analysis is based on Iraqi prisoner of war reports. According to the Project on Defense Alternatives, between 20,000 and 26,000 Iraqi military personnel were killed in the conflict while 75,000 others were wounded.

Iraqi Casualties for Operation Iraqi Freedom

Credible estimates of Iraq War casualties range from 150,000 to 460,000. Other disputed estimates, such as the 2006 Lancet study, and the 2007 Opinion Research Business survey, put the numbers as high as 650,000 and 1.2 million respectively, while body counts, which likely underestimate mortality, put the numbers as low as 110,000.

Scientific surveys:

Source	Estimated Violent Deaths	Time Period
Iraq Family Health Survey	151,000 Violent Deaths	March 2003 to June 2006
Lancent Survey	601,027 Violent Deaths out of 654,965 Excess Deaths	March 2003 to June 2006

MAXIM #8

LESSON LEARNED

The battlefields throughout history are littered by amateur soldiers who did not respect the lethality of professional armies.

Future Combatant in Training

Civilian terrorist throwing a burning Molotov cocktail

MAXIM #9

FRIENDLY FIRE ISN'T

Fratricide, as defined by the U.S. Army Training and Doctrine Command, is the employment of friendly weapons and munitions with the intent to kill the enemy or destroy his equipment or facilities which results in unforeseen and unintentional death or injury to friendly personnel. As such, friendly fire isn't—or when the pin is pulled, Mr. Grenade is no longer our friend.

It is an especially severe problem in coalition warfare, where not all participants are familiar with one another, or may not have fully interoperable communications and navigation. Both in the Second World War and the Vietnam War, 15-20% of US casualties were the result of fratricide. In the 1990 Gulf War, which had an even higher operational tempo and more participants, the rate had increased to 24%. It is by no means limited to the US; "Britain has historically been one of the worst offenders. In 1471, during the War of the Roses, the Lancastrian division fired on its forces by mistake. During the Second Word War, on September 10, 1939, the submarine *HMS Triton* sank fellow Royal Navy submarine *HMS Oxley* and, in the 1982 Falklands War, *HMS Cardiff* shot down a friendly Gazelle helicopter."

MAXIM #9

FRIENDLY FIRE ISN'T

Painting of the Battle of Chancellorsville May 2nd, 1863, the Wounding of Lieutenant General Thomas J. "Stonewall" Jackson by Kurz & Allison, 1889

When war broke out in 1861, Thomas Jackson, a West Point graduate and former artillery instructor at the Virginia Military Institute, became a Brigadier General in the Confederate Army and commanded five regiments raised in Virginia's Shenandoah Valley. At the Battle of Bull Run in July 1861, Jackson earned distinction by leading the attack to bridge a gap that secured the defensive line against the Union attack. Confederate General Barnard Bee, upon noting Jackson's audacious charge and trying to inspire his troops, exclaimed, "There stands Jackson like a stone wall," and thus provided one of the most enduring nicknames in history.

By 1862, Jackson was now a Major General and recognized as one of the most effective commanders in the Confederate army. Leading his force on one of the most brilliant campaigns in military history during the summer of 1862, Jackson marched around the Shenandoah Valley and held off three Union armies while providing relief for Confederates pinned down on the James Peninsula by George McClellan's army. He later rejoined the Army of Northern Virginia for the Seven Days battles, and his leadership was stellar at Second Bull Run in August 1862. He soon became Lee's most trusted corps commander.

At the Battle of Chancellorsville, both General Lee and Jackson faced an army twice the size of theirs. Lee daringly split his force and sent Jackson around the Union flank—a move that resulted in perhaps the Army of the Potomac's most stunning defeat of the war. When nightfall halted the attack, Jackson rode forward to reconnoiter the territory for another assault. But as he and his aides rode back to the lines, a group of Rebels opened fire. Jackson was hit three times, and a Southern bullet shattered his left arm, which had to be amputated the next day. Soon, pneumonia set in, and Jackson began to fade. He died, as he had wished, on the Sabbath, May 10, 1863, with these last words: "Let us cross over the river and rest under the shade of the trees."

MAXIM #9

FRIENDLY FIRE ISN'T

Iron Mike Statue – Commemorating U.S. Airborne Soldiers
U.S. Airborne Soldiers Exiting Aircraft

Operation Codename "Husky" – Began on July 9, 1943 when 2,200 American paratroopers led by Colonel James Gavin of the 505th Parachute Infantry Regiment of the 82nd Airborne Division parachuted in Gela, Sicily. The following day, another 170,000 allied troops landed at Sicily, which became the largest amphibious operation to that point in American history.

On July 11, 1943, 144 C-47 and C–53 aircraft transported Colonel Reuben Tucker's 504th Parachute Infantry Regiment of the 82nd Airborne Division to further exploit the Allied advance. An order was issued to naval commanders that there would be American paratrooper transports flying overhead but, unfortunately, many naval crewmen stated that they were unaware of the order.

Although the first two transport planes followed their prescribed course and dropped their paratroopers on target, the following formation was mistaken as enemy aircraft and, as such, received intensive fire.

The US Army's official history reads, "The slow-flying, majestic columns of aircraft were like sitting ducks." Dozens of transport planes were hit. One exploded in mid-air. Another, on fire, tried to ditch to save the paratroopers. Squadrons broke apart, tried to reform, and scattered again. Eight pilots turned back for Tunisia still carrying their paratroopers. Those over Sicily dropped paratroopers wherever they could. Some of the jumpers descended into the sea and drowned. Some were killed by friendly fire while dangling from their chutes in the night sky. One transport plane caught fire and headed down, veering sharply to avoid hitting an Allied ship. Careening across the water, the plane trailed a long orange plume of flame as men, some of them on fire, rained from the fuselage.

At the time, the shoot-down over Gela was the worst friendly-fire incident in US history. A total of 318 American soldiers were killed or wounded (including Brigadier General Charles L. Keerans Jr the Assistant Division Commander of the 82nd Airborne Division). Twenty-three transport planes failed to return; others limped back to Tunisia badly damaged, one riddled with over 1,000 bullet holes; many landed with blood all over the floorboards.

MAXIM #9

FRIENDLY FIRE ISN'T

Marshal Murat – OCT 13, 1815 – "Spare my face, aim at the heart."

Marshal Joachim Murat (1767–1815) was one of Napoleon's most flamboyant and dashing cavalry commanders. He distinguished himself in several campaigns in Italy, Egypt, the Wars of the Third and Fourth Coalition. Napoleon ultimately rewarded Murat for his bold generalship by appointing him the King of Naples on

August 1, 1808. He later participated in the Russian Campaign in 1813, fighting in several key battles such as Ostrovno, Krasnvi, Smolensk, Valutino and Borodino. After the massive French defeat at Leipzig Germany in 1813, where he commanded 12,000 cavalrymen, he returned to Naples and in 1814 he officially changed sides, allying himself with Napoleon's opponents. When Napoleon returned from exile at the start of the Hundred Days in 1815, he refused to offer Murat a military command during the Waterloo campaign, a serious mistake that greatly reduced the effectiveness of his cavalry at Waterloo. After Napoleon's second abdication, Murat was offered asylum in Austria. However, he decided to make one last bid for power. He raised a force of 250 soldiers on Corsica and attempted to cross over to Calabria. A storm scattered his fleet, and he found himself isolated at Pizzo. Shortly thereafter, he was captured and arrested by the Bourbans, condemned by a court-martial and executed for disturbing the peace on October 13, 1815.

MAXIM #9

FRIENDLY FIRE ISN'T

During service in the Second Boer War, Lieutenant Henry "Breaker" Harboard Morant participated participated in the summary execution of several Boer (Afrikaner) prisoners and the killing of a German missionary, Daniel Heese, who had been a witness to the shootings. His actions led to his controversial court-martial and execution for murder.

Shortly before 06:00 hours, Morant and Handcock were led out of the fort at Pretoria to be executed by a firing squad from

Henry Harboard – 1902 – Australian Hero and Poet of Breaker Morant fame seated by his dog: "Shoot straight, you bastards, and don't make a mess of it."

the Cameron Highlanders. Both men refused to be blindfolded; Morant gave his cigarette case to the squad leader, and his famous last words were: "Shoot straight, you bastards! Don't make a mess of it!" A contemporary report (from The Argus 3 April 1902), however, has his last words as, "Take this thing (the blindfold) off," and on its removal, "Be sure and make a good job of it!" Witton wrote that he was by then at Pretoria railway station and heard the volley of shots that killed his comrades. However, Poore, who attended the execution, wrote in his diary that he put Witton and Lieutenant Picton on the train that left at 17:30 hours. Thus, Witton would have been several miles on the way to Cape Town when the execution occurred.

MAXIM #9

FRIENDLY FIRE ISN'T

Photo of Robert Childers

Robert Erskine Childers (DSC) (June 25, 1870–November 24, 1922) was a well decorated soldier during the Gallipoli Campaign in 1915 and earned the coveted Distinguished Service Cross in 1916. He also wrote the influential novel **The Riddle of the Sands.**

As a staunch Irish nationalist, he was arrested on November 10, 1923 for smuggling guns to Ireland during the Irish Civil War. He was tried and ultimately convicted for possessing a Spanish made 32 caliber pistol and sentenced to death.

Before his execution, in the spirit of reconciliation, Childers shook hands with each member of the firing squad and further, obtained a promise from his then 16-year old son, the future President Erskine Hamilton Childers, to seek out and shake the hand of every man who had signed his father's death warrant. His last words, spoken to them, were "Take a step or two forward, lads. It will be easier that way."

On November 24, 1923, Childers was executed by firing squad at the Beggar's Bush Barracks in Dublin, Ireland.

Éamon de Valera said of him, "He died the Prince he was. Of all the men I ever met, I would say he was the noblest."

MAXIM #9
LESSON LEARNED

Fratricide is something to be prevented. Fratricide is a subset of deconfliction and is the part of the mission planning process that tries to ensure that all pre-planned attacks know the position of friendly forces. One of the drivers of network-centric warfare is giving all units and personnel improved situational awareness, such that a unit that moves to take advantage of a sudden enemy weakness is not incorrectly identified as an enemy force to be engaged.

Fratricide against one's own troops has a variety of causes. In a fast-moving battlefield, perhaps the most common cause is improper identification. It is worth noting that use of identification-friend-or-foe technology preceded the common use of the terms "friendly fire" or "fratricide." Positive identification is a major preventive step.

Formally, the United States Department of Defense defines "friendly fire" as "In casualty reporting, a casualty circumstance applicable to persons killed in action or wounded in action mistakenly or accidentally by friendly forces actively engaged with the enemy, who are directing fire at a hostile force or what is thought to be a hostile force."

Remains of a WWI German Soldier outside his dugout at Beaumont Hamel, Nov 1916

MAXIM #10

MAKE IT TOO TOUGH FOR THE ENEMY TO GET IN, AND YOU WON'T BE ABLE TO GET OUT!

Eben-Emael was a Belgian fortress between Liège and Maastricht, near the Albert Canal, defending the Belgian-German border. Constructed in 1931–1935, it was reputed to be impregnable and, at the time, the largest in the world. But on 10 May 1940, 78 paratroopers of the German 7th *Flieger* (later 1st *Fallschirmjäger* Division) landed on the fortress with gliders (type DFS 230), armed with special high explosives to damage the fortress and its guns. As the fortress had no defense against air-attacks or machinegun positions, one day later, when they were reinforced by the German 151st Infantry Regiment, at 13:30 Hours on 11 May, the fortress surrendered. Twelve hundred Belgian soldiers were captured.

Eben-Emael, an underground fort, was Belgium's hope to defend its eastern borders from invasion, charged with defending or destroying three key bridges. It also gave protection to the south of what was called the *Gap of Vise*. A fortress to protect this approach to Liège had been conceived in the latter 19th century, but only became politically convincing after the Albert Canal was dug (to provide a route for Belgian river transport that did not require entering Dutch territory). Thus, the fortress was only completed in 1935, being sited between the river and the canal that bypassed it. With its steel and concrete cupolas, Fort Eben-Emael was thought to be impenetrable.

However, the Germans had planned the capture of the fort well in advance. In preparation, they had practiced assaulting a full-scale mock up of the fort's exterior in occupied Czechoslovakia using the recently built and captured Beneš Wall that was modeled to a large degree on the western designs. Adolf Hitler himself conceived of a plan to take over the fort using gliders (it would have been difficult and messy to parachute a large number of men into the small area) and utilizing the new top secret shaped charge (also called "hollow charge") bombs to penetrate the cupolas.

Good espionage and superior planning, combined with unpreparedness on the Belgian side, helped make the May 10, 1940 execution of Hitler's top secret plan a swift and overwhelming success. The capture of Eben-Emael involved the first utilization of gliders for the initial attack and the first use of hollow charge devices in war. The gliders led by First Lieutenant Rudolf Witzig landed on the "roof" of the fortress. There they were able to use the hollow charges to destroy or disable the gun cupolas. They also used a flamethrower against machine guns. The Belgians did destroy one of the key bridges, preventing it from being used by the Germans but also preventing a relieving force from aiding the fortress.

After its capture, the fort was evaluated for use as an underground factory for the V-1 rocket, but production was never undertaken.

MAXIM #10

MAKE IT TOO TOUGH FOR THE ENEMY TO GET IN, AND YOU WON'T BE ABLE TO GET OUT!

Vercingetorix, the statue of a famous Gaul warrior who defied the Roman Emperor, Julius Caesar, Alesia France

Prelude to the Siege of Alesia:

Having been appointed governor of the Roman province of Gallia Narbonensis (modern Provence) in 58 BC, Julius Caesar proceeded to conquer the Gallic tribes over the next few years, maintaining control through a careful divide and rule strategy. He exploited the factionalism among the Gallic elites by favoring certain noblemen over others via political support and such luxuries as Roman wine and refined clothing.

By 52 BC, Julius Caesar, commanding the seemingly invincible Roman legions, had nearly subjugated the entire territory of Gaul (present-day Belgium and France). Realizing the immediate need to dislodge the Roman invaders from their homeland, the once fractious tribes of Gaul convened a council and selected a new king and chieftain named Vercingetorix, a 30-year old charismatic warrior/nobleman hailing from the Averni tribe.

Vercingetorix, equipped with the requisite sense of urgency, quickly marshaled his forces and adopted an effective scorched earth strategy consisting of continual harassment of the enemy while retreating to natural fortifications and burning towns and agricultural fields in the process. As such, Caesar's forces were deprived of precious resources as well as a safe haven and their predicament had, thus, became increasingly perilous.

MAXIM #10

MAKE IT TOO TOUGH FOR THE ENEMY TO GET IN, AND YOU WON'T BE ABLE TO GET OUT!

Prelude to the Siege of Alesia continued:

Wanting to exploit the weakness of the now beleaguered Roman legions, Vercingetorix then engaged and crushed Caesar's hard-pressed legions at the Battle of Gergovia. Caesar, after losing several thousands of soldiers, was then ignominiously forced to withdraw his units.

Ultimately, however, the Romans consolidated and re-equipped their forces and then soundly defeated the Gauls near Divio. Vercingetorix, along with a force of 80,000 men, came to the harsh realization that they were no match in open battle against the 60,000 Roman Legionaries and their Germanic cavalry allied force and, thus, retreated in late September 52 BC to the fortified hilltop town of Alesia.

Caesar, still mindful of his force's recent defeat at Gergovia, decided rather than to conduct a costly direct assault against a well-fortified enemy position that commanded the heights, that he would fare better by hemming the Gauls inside the fort (a circumvallation strategy) in order to starve them out. Caesar, in his commentaries, suggests that food was scarce prior to the fall harvest and surmised that the Gauls only had about 30 days' food to feed their army.

The Siege of Alesia, 52. BC

In less than three weeks' time, Caesar's industrious engineers constructed a timber and earthen wall surrounding the town of Alesia. The wall measured an impressive 11 miles in length by 12 feet in height and was accompanied by a wide ditch dug out in front of the work and a second water-filled trench behind it.

The Gauls, in reactive fashion, deployed several raiding parities to disrupt the Roman effort but to no avail and Vercingetorix, realizing that there were still some gaps in the unfinished Roman wall, ordered some of his cavalry to attempt a breakout under cover of darkness to escape to nearby tribes and call upon them to help lift the siege. However, some deserters and captured cavalrymen notified Caesar of Vercingetorix's plan and he ordered the construction of a second rampart, this time facing outward to form a wall of contravallation. The outer wall was similar to the inner wall but was longer; i.e. 15 miles in length and which left enough of a gap in between to fortify the entire Roman army and to protect them from sally attempts by Vercingetorix as well as the relief army that was certain to come to the aid of the besieged defenders.

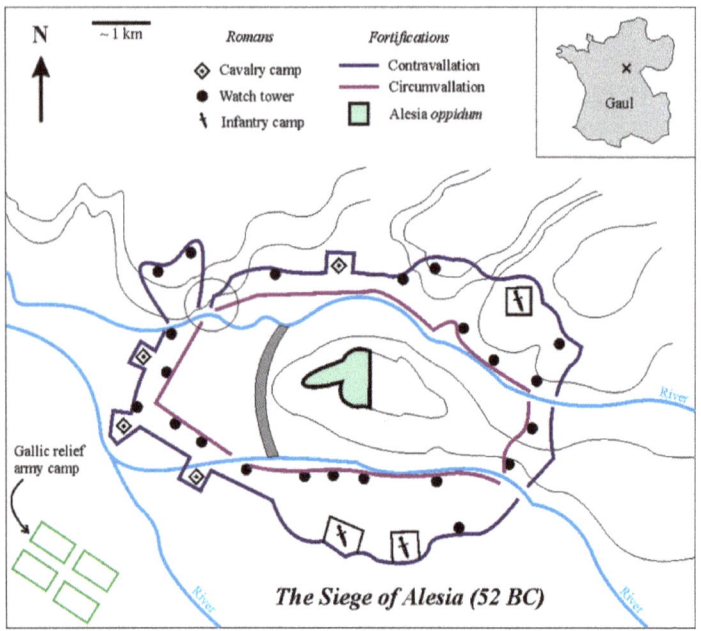

MAXIM #10

MAKE IT TOO TOUGH FOR THE ENEMY TO GET IN, AND YOU WON'T BE ABLE TO GET OUT!

The Siege of Alesia, 52 BC continued:

While waiting for the relief force, Vercingetorix, with an estimated 180,000 people (including women and children), were desperately short of food and were on the verge of surrendering. Vercingetorix, as a delay tactic, then opened up the fortress gates hoping that Caesar would be chivalrous and allow them to pass through the battle lines toward safety. However, Caesar, sensing the ploy and being a calloused practitioner of "Total War," refused them passage. The women and children were therefore forced to camp between the two armies and slowly starved. For those cavalrymen that did escape, they managed to rally support for Vercingetorix by recruiting a massive army of 250,000 Gauls (most modern historians estimate that the number was likely closer to 100,000 troops) and reached the besieged fortress in late September in 52 BC.

The battle began with a charge from the Gauls on the exterior of the Roman fortifications. A hard-fought engagement from noon to sunset ensued, with neither side having a clear advantage. Both Romans and Gauls fought with equal valor and inspired by the fight, Vercingetorix led his men out of Alesia toward the inner Roman wall. Unable to penetrate the defenses, he was not able to lend support to his countrymen, and eventually Caesar's Germanic cavalry turned the Gallic flank and sent them back to their camps.

At midnight of the following day, the Gauls outside the Roman work, equipped with ladders, hooks and equipment for scaling walls, launched their attack in concert with Vercingetorix, who launched a simultaneous attack from the inner walls. Despite the Gauls' initial success and killing several hundred Romans, they were ultimately forced to retreat due to superior Roman artillery.

On October 2nd, sometime around mid-day, a reconnaissance party under the command of Vergasillaunus discovered a weakness in the Roman lines. Because of natural obstructions, the probing force discovered that there were areas in the defense works where walls simply couldn't be built. As such, over 60,000 Gauls launched a simultaneous attack on both sides of the Roman works and thus threatened to rout the outnumbered Romans. Caesar, realizing their precarious position, thrust himself directly into the thick of battle and inspired his troops to hold their lines. He then, along with 13 cohorts, left the relative safety of the walls and rode outside to attack the Gauls from the rear while his other officer, Labienus, engaged the enemy from the front. The Gauls, now trapped between both Roman forces, were routed and fled the battlefield. The Germanic cavalry, in hot pursuit of the fleeing Gauls, managed to then virtually annihilate the remaining force.

Aftermath:

Forced back into Alesia after the defeat of his relief force, with no hope of additional reinforcements, and only with the starving remnants of his own army, Vercingetorix was forced to surrender. Caesar sat at the head of his lines and waited for the approach of the Gallic chieftains. Vercingetorix and his fellow leaders laid down their arms and surrendered quietly, where he was eventually led away to Rome. He would sit and rot in a Roman prison for five miserable years, awaiting the day when Caesar could have his triumph, to be followed by the ritual execution of the enemy leader. As a reward Caesar's men each received one Gallic slave in addition to monetary spoils of war.

Vercingetorix Throws Down His Arms at the Feet of Julius Caesar painted by Lionel Noel Royer – 1899

MAXIM #10

MAKE IT TOO TOUGH FOR THE ENEMY TO GET IN, AND YOU WON'T BE ABLE TO GET OUT!

Greek Trireme boats at the Siege of Tyre 332 BC

The **Siege of Tyre**, a strategic coastal base on the Mediterranean Sea, was orchestrated by Alexander the Great in 332 BC during his campaigns against the Persians. The Macedonian army was unable to capture the city through conventional means because it was on an island and had walls right up to the sea. Alexander responded to this problem by first blockading and besieging Tyre for seven months, and then by building a causeway that allowed him to breach the fortifications.

It is said that Alexander was so enraged at the Tyrians' defense and the loss of his men that he destroyed half the city. According to Arrian, 8,000 Tyrian civilians were massacred after the city fell. Alexander granted pardon to the king and his family, whilst the 30,000 residents and foreigners taken were sold into slavery.

As Alexander could not attack the city from the sea, he built a kilometer-long causeway stretching out to the island on a natural land bridge no more than two meters deep.

This causeway allowed his artillery to get in range of the walls, and is still there to this day, as it was made of stone. As the work came near the walls, however, the water became much deeper, and the combined attacks from the walls and Tyrian navy made construction nearly impossible. Therefore, Alexander constructed two towers 50 m (160 ft) high and moved them to the end of the causeway. Like most of Alexander's siege towers, these were moving artillery platforms, with catapults on the top to clear defenders off the walls, and ballista below to hurl rocks at the wall and attacking ships. The towers were made of wood but were covered in rawhide to protect them from fire arrows. Although these towers were possibly the largest of their kind ever made, the Tyrians quickly devised a counterattack. They used an old horse transport ship, filling it with dried branches, pitch, sulfur, and various other combustibles. They then hung cauldrons of oil from the masts, so that they would fall onto the deck once the masts burned through. They also weighed down the back of the ship so that the front rose above the water. They then lit it on fire and ran it up onto the causeway. The fire spread quickly, engulfing both towers and the other siege equipment that had been brought up. The Tyrian ships swarmed the pier, destroying any siege equipment that hadn't caught fire, and driving off Macedonian crews that were trying to put out the fires.

MAXIM #10

MAKE IT TOO TOUGH FOR THE ENEMY TO GET IN, AND YOU WON'T BE ABLE TO GET OUT!

Statue of Alexander the Great, Thessaloniki, Greece

Alexander was convinced that he would not be able to take Tyre without a navy. However, the Persian navy returned to find their home cities under Alexander's control. The Persians' allegiance to their cities allowed Alexander to command 80 ships. This coincided with the arrival of another 120 from Cyprus, which had heard of his victories and wished to join him. With the arrival of another 23 ships, Alexander had 223 galleys under his command. Alexander then sailed on Tyre and quickly blockaded both ports with his superior numbers. He had several of the slower galleys, and a few barges, refit with battering rams. Finding that large underwater blocks of stone kept the rams from reaching the walls, Alexander had them removed by crane ships. The rams then anchored near the walls, but the Tyrians sent out ships and divers to cut the anchor cables. Alexander responded by replacing them with chains. The Tyrians launched another counterattack, yet were not so fortunate this time. They noticed that Alexander returned to the mainland at the same time every afternoon for lunch, at the same time much of his navy did. They therefore attacked at this time, but found Alexander had skipped his afternoon nap, and was able to quickly counter the sortie.

Conclusion of the siege

Alexander started testing the wall at various points with his rams, until he made a small breach in the south end of the island. He then coordinated an attack across the breach with a bombardment from all sides by his navy. Alexander is said to have personally taken part in the attack on the city, fighting from the top of a siege tower. Once his troops forced their way into the city, they easily overtook the garrison, and quickly captured the city. Those citizens that took shelter in the temple of Melkart were pardoned by Alexander, including the king of Tyre. According to Quintus Curtius Rufus, 6,000 fighting men were killed within the city and 2,000 Tyrians were crucified on the beach. The others, some 30,000 people, were sold into slavery. The severity of reprisals was both because of the length of the siege, and because the Tyrians had executed some captured soldiers on the walls, in sight of the attackers.

MAXIM #10
LESSON LEARNED

Sun Tzu – Do not completely encircle your enemy or he will likely fight to the death.

Retreat of the Ten Thousand, at Cunaxa fought between t he Persians & 10,000 Greek mercenaries of Cyrus the Young 401 BC Jean Adrien Guignet – (1816–1854)

The Ten Thousand were a band of Greek mercenaries hired by the Persian prince Cyrus the Younger to wage a civil war against his brother, King Artaxerxes II, 401 BC.

MAXIM #11

THE ONE ITEM THAT YOU NEED IS ALWAYS IN SHORT SUPPLY

Ike Clanton – 1881 OK Corral "Good, God won't someone give me some more cartridges for a last shot?"

Doc Holliday and Wyatt Earp walking enroute to the O.K. Corral

Joseph Isaac (Ike) Clanton (1847–June 1, 1887) was a member of a group of outlaws known as The Cowboys that had ongoing conflicts with lawmen Wyatt, Virgil, Morgan Earp and Wyatt's friend Doc Holliday due to disputes over the town's gambling business. On October 26, 1881, Ike was present at the Gunfight at the O.K. Corral in the boomtown of Tombstone, Arizona Territory, but was unarmed and ran from the gunfight. His 19-year-old brother Billy was killed in the gunfight. Ike filed murder charges against the Earps but after a 30-day preliminary hearing, Justice Wells Spicer ruled that there was not enough evidence to indict them. Ike was implicated in the attempted assassination of Virgil Earp on December 30, 1881 but was released for lack of evidence. Ike died in the saddle six years later when he was shot by a lawman pursuing him on cattle-rustling charges.

MAXIM #11

THE ONE ITEM THAT YOU NEED IS ALWAYS IN SHORT SUPPLY

Pickett's Charge, Battle of Gettysburg, July 3, 1863, Encyclopedia Britannica

Confederate States Army Brigadier General, Lewis Armistead – "Give them cold steel men" – Gettysburg 1863 after running out of ammo. Bayonets and sword attack.

MAXIM #11

THE ONE ITEM THAT YOU NEED IS ALWAYS IN SHORT SUPPLY

Photo of abandoned German tanks in action, WWII

Joseph Stalin once said: *"The war was decided by engines and octane."*

Winston Churchill agreed with Stalin on the importance of fuel: *"Above all, petrol governed every movement."*

The German Logistics Nightmare:

Fuel shortages had severely damaging consequences on the German armed forces in World War II. In some cases, Hitler and the German High Command had to change their entire war strategies because of the fuel situation.

Take for example the German summer offensive of 1942. German Army Group South was split into two parts. Army Group A was to advance into the Caucasus to seize its oil fields, while Army Group B advanced to the Volga River and Stalingrad to cover Army Group A's left flank.

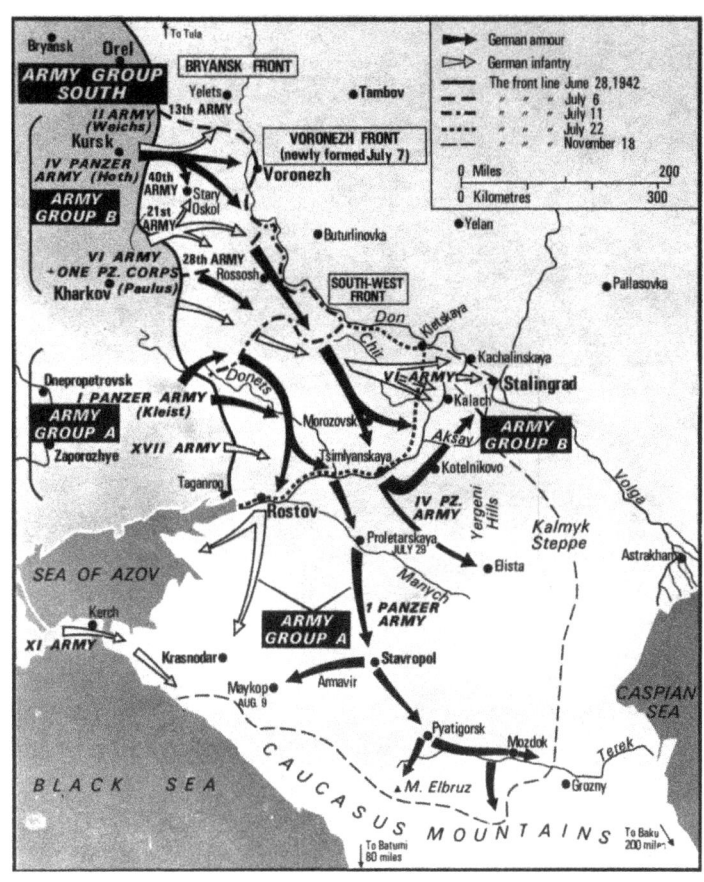

German Offensive Sketch 1942, WWII

MAXIM #11

THE ONE ITEM THAT YOU NEED IS ALWAYS IN SHORT SUPPLY

The German Logistics Nightmare:

Bear in mind that the initial primary target of the German invasion was Moscow, and Hitler had expected to capture Moscow in the first 3-4 months of the war. But as the Wehrmacht failed to take Moscow in 1941 and the war became one of attrition, the Germans had to revise their strategy since they simply didn't have enough fuel for the German war machine. Reliance on the oil fields of Romania and Hungary were insufficient and too far to make it logistically practical.

Accordingly, in 1942, Hitler halted all major offensives in northern (Leningrad) and central Russia (Moscow), and instead concentrated his effort on the south to seize the Soviet oil fields.

This strategy failed spectacularly. Army Group B was annihilated in the Stalingrad meat grinder. After months of fierce fighting in the mountains, Army Group A had managed to capture only 1 out of 9 major Soviet oil fields at Maikop, but it was so thoroughly trashed by the retreating Soviet forces that two years of reconstruction was needed to put it back to normal operation. When the German forces were compelled to hurriedly withdraw from Maikop in January 1943 in order to avoid being cut off after the fall of Stalingrad, Germany had failed to obtain a single drop of Caucasian oil.

Then in late 1944 as the Soviet army was enroute to seize the Hungarian oil refineries, Hitler redeployed two elite SS Panzer Corps from Poland to the south to secure his last oil supply, since Romania had then switched sides to support the Allies in September 1944. In effect, if Hitler had not had to concern himself about the lack of oil supplies it is quite likely that the Soviet Vistula-Oder offensive in Poland would have met with much fiercer resistance and delayed General Zhukov's capture of Warsaw, which capitulated after only five days of fighting.

In December 1944, the Third Reich launched one last daring counteroffensive, Operation Mist, famously known as the Ardennes Offensive or the Battle of the Bulge, in an attempt to push the Allied front line west from northern France to northwestern Belgium. Despite the Nazis setting aside 5 million gallons for this battle to fuel their dreaded Panzer and Tiger tanks and planning to capture American fuel depots during their advance, the German army's effort fell short due to a variety of reasons, including poor road conditions, logical missteps and the Allied evacuating forces destroying millions of gallons of gas to prevent its use by the enemy. Owing to the critical shortage of oil, the German infantry divisions resorted to using some 50,000 horses to transport personnel and equipment in the Ardennes and by the end of Christmas, many German tanks were running on fumes and were unable to continue the advance across the Meuse River. By mid-January 1945, the counterattack had crumbled, and the Allies had successfully erased the "Bulge" in their lines and pushed the Germans back to their original positions.

Photo of 703rd Tank Destroyer Battalion, 3rd Armored Division passes Panzer IV of Panzer Abteilung 115, 15 Panzer Grenadier Division Langla-1944

MAXIM #11

LESSON LEARNED

Large Weapons Cache Afghanistan

"My logisticians are a humorless lot...they know if my campaign fails, they are the first ones I will slay." – Alexander

"The line between disorder and order lies in logistics... Victorious warriors win first and then go to war." – Sun Tzu

"There is nothing more common than to find considerations of supply affecting the strategic lines of a campaign and a war." – General Carl von Clausewitz

"Logistics is the stuff that if you don't have enough of, the war will not be won as soon as." – General Nathaniel Green, Quartermaster, American Revolutionary Army

"The amateurs discuss tactics; the professionals discuss logistics." – Napoleon Bonaparte

"Gentlemen, the officer who doesn't know his communications and supply as well as his tactics is totally useless." – General George S. Patton, U.S. Army

"Leaders win through logistics. Vision, sure. Strategy, yes. But when you go to war, you need to have both toilet paper and bullets at the right place at the right time. In other words, you must win through superior logistics." – Tom Peters- Rule #3 in "Leadership is Confusing As Hell," Fast Company, March 2001.

MAXIM #12

MILITARY INTELLIGENCE IS A CONTRADICTION

Masked cyber terrorist in military uniform hacking army intelligence, February 12, 2017

"Hey Private, where in the hell were you at Camouflage practice yesterday?" – Answer "Thank you, Drill Sergeant!"

MAXIM #12

MILITARY INTELLIGENCE IS A CONTRADICTION

Korean War Veterans Memorial, Washington, D.C.

The American intelligence community's experience with the People's Republic of China and North Korea began with a disaster, a catastrophic intelligence failure in 1950 that cost the lives of thousands of Americans. Worse, it was a self-imposed disaster—the result of terrible intelligence management, not the poor collection or analysis of information. To add insult to injury, the government of India had warned the United States that disaster loomed but was ignored.

Advance on the Yalu River, 1950. On September 15, 1950, the troops under the command of General of the Army Douglas MacArthur, CinC of the UN Command since July 10, landed at Inchon. The landing followed a surprise attack by Kim Il Sung's Communist North on June 25, which had all but defeated the South Koreans, and the handful of Americans rushed from Japan to support them.

One of warfare's most inspired amphibious operations, Inchon caught the North Koreans completely off-balance and changed the course of the Korean War. By the beginning of October, MacArthur's victorious forces were pursuing a broken enemy across the 38th parallel. Brimming over with hubris and determined to smash the Communist forces once and for all, MacArthur convinced President Harry S Truman to allow him to proceed to the Yalu River, the sensitive border with both the People's Republic of China and the Soviet Union. This despite receiving intelligence from India that China would likely intervene as well as the alarms raised by then-CIA director Admiral Roscoe Hillenkoetter.

Undetected by Western Intelligence, hundreds of thousands of Chinese soldiers began infiltrating by night, with great skill, across the Yalu. As the UN forces moved north from Pyongyang, MacArthur's commander, General Walker, found himself heading with a mixed force of 100,000 men into rugged, wintry country, and covering a front several times wider than the much more defensible 38th parallel.

Inevitably, the force became divided. On November 25, as Walker was preparing his final blow, the Chinese struck with devastating force along the Chongchon Valley, with eight armies of thirty divisions, totaling more than 300,000 men, several times the available strength of the UN forces. It was a great ambush.

Walker's right wing crumpled. Swiftly, the line buckled, and MacArthur's troops, in an unparalleled reversal of fortune, reeled back to the 38th parallel. For the US forces caught up in the "bug-out" in appalling winter conditions, it was one of the worst defeats in American history.

Thirteen thousand casualties were suffered in withdrawal, and the legendary, untouchable, invincible MacArthur was sacked a few months later. But the longer-term consequences were far greater. The Korean War could no longer be won, by either side, and would drag on for another two and a half bitter years, costing 54,000 American lives and many more Koreans and Chinese. The PRC became a major power.

MAXIM #12

MILITARY INTELLIGENCE IS A CONTRADICTION

Painting of British surrender to the Ottomans at Kut-El-Amara on April 29, 2016, World War I. National Army Museum, Chelsea, London, NAM Accession # NAM.1960-09-35-2

The Siege of Kut – British Indian 6th Division's attempt to capture Baghdad by underestimating the strength of the Ottoman forces met unexpected heavy resistance. They were defeated at the Battle of Ctesiphon and besieged in Kut Al Amara. Despite relief efforts by British troops, Kut surrendered to Ottoman Forces on 29 April 1916, ending in the capture of General Townshend himself, many high-ranked British officers, and 11,000 soldiers. Around 30,000 casualties had also been suffered. This battle is considered one of the most humiliating defeats of the British army.

MAXIM #12
MILITARY INTELLIGENCE IS A CONTRADICTION

Australian ANZAC Soldiers on Patrol - Gallipoli, Turkey

WWI Turkish infantryman statue at Gallipoli, Turkey

The Gallipoli campaign, which cost the lives of tens of thousands of Allied soldiers, lasted from April 1915 to January 1918 and was doomed from the very beginning. Too few soldiers were allocated to the landings. To compound this, the Allied intelligence services failed to provide adequate intelligence. For example, they failed to indicate that Gallipoli was not suitable for large-scale landings because of the nature of the terrain. Then the entire operation was poorly planned with little forethought from logistics or what the allies would do if the Turks were waiting for the invaders at the proposed beachheads. Then there was a complete failure to recognize that the Turks would fight fiercely because they were fighting for their homeland, symbolized by the great leadership displayed by the future Ataturk at Sulva Bay and elsewhere. In effect, although the German commander at Gallipoli devised a clever strategy, he was greatly assisted by the utter failings of the Allies.

MAXIM #12
MILITARY INTELLIGENCE IS A CONTRADICTION

Che Guevara Victory Portrait – Bay of Pigs

The Bay of Pigs Invasion was a failed military invasion of Cuba undertaken by the Central Intelligence Agency of the United States on April 17, 1961 and attempted to overthrow Cuban President Fidel Castro with 1,500 Cuban exiles. Not only were the exiles heavily outnumbered when they reached the bay, but the US-promised air support never came to aid the exiles.

In November 1961, CIA Inspector-General Lyman B. Kirkpatrick authored a report, 'Survey of the Cuban Operation,' that remained classified until 1998. The conclusions were:
1. The C.I.A. exceeded its capabilities in developing the project from guerrilla support to overt armed action without any plausible deniability.
2. The organization failed to realistically assess risks and to adequately communicate information and decisions internally and with other government principals.
3. There was insufficient involvement between the CIA and the exiled leaders.
4. The spy agency failed to sufficiently organize internal resistance in Cuba and, moreover, lacked stable policies and or contingency plans if matters went awry.
5. The CIA failed to competently collect and analyze intelligence about Cuban forces.
6. The organization suffered from poor internal management and junior staff members regularly failed to adequately communicate with one another as well as with the exiled leaders. Further, there was a manifest lack of a high-quality experienced staff who would have immediately recognized that the operation from the onset lacked a sufficient number of Spanish speakers, training facilities and material resources needed to conduct a successful mission.

MAXIM #12
LESSON LEARNED

According to Gregory Elder's article **Intelligence in War: It Can Be Decisive**, reference CIA report, Volume 50, #2, force and its employment are significant in driving outcomes in combat. However, it is operational and tactical intelligence, not necessarily numbers, technology, or tactics, that can have the most decisive impact on how forces are employed and how success is achieved in wartime operations. History repeatedly has demonstrated that numerically inferior forces, armed with less capable technologies, can win when leaders are armed with accurate intelligence they believe they can act upon. Such intelligence can be a force multiplier. Therefore, considering the value of force employment, technology, and mass without placing a corresponding value on intelligence is a mistake.

Now the reason the enlightened prince and the wise general conquer the enemy whenever they move and their achievements surpass those of ordinary men is foreknowledge. – Sun Tzu, The Art of War

Secret nuclear bunker sign, Essex England

MAXIM #13

IF YOU'RE SHORT OF EVERYTHING BUT THE ENEMY, YOU'RE IN A COMBAT ZONE

Painting of The Defense of Rorke's Drift by Alphonse de Neuville, 1880

The Battle of Rorke's Drift was a battle in the Anglo-Zulu War. The defense of the mission station of Rorke's Drift immediately followed the British army's defeat at the Battle of Isandlwana earlier that morning on 22 January 1879, and continued to the following day, 23 January. One hundred and thirty-nine British soldiers successfully defended their garrison against an intense assault by four to five thousand Zulu warriors. The overwhelming Zulu attack on Rorke's Drift came very close to defeating the tiny British garrison, and the British success is held as one of history's finest defenses. Eleven Victoria Crosses were awarded to the defenders, along with a number of other decorations and honors.

MAXIM #13

IF YOU'RE SHORT OF EVERYTHING BUT THE ENEMY, YOU'RE IN A COMBAT ZONE

Charging Chariots of the Persian Army by André Castaigne – (1861–1921)

During the summer of 331 BC, Alexander, with a force of 40,000 infantry and 7,000 cavalry, set out from Tyre with the intention of finding and crushing the Persian King Darius III and his Imperial army once and for all. Desperate to halt the Macedonian advance, Darius scoured his empire for resources and men and ultimately amassed a vast array of troops of numerous nationalities from all over his empire. Although the reports vary, the Greek historian Arrian places the strength of the Persian army at 1,000,000 infantry, 40,000 cavalry, 200 scythe chariots and several elephants. Darius then assembled his forces near Arbela and chose a wide plain for the battlefield since he believed that it would better facilitate the use of his chariots and elephants and would allow him to envelop the entire Macedonian army.

After crossing the Tigris River, Alexander learned from scouts of the presence of a Persian cavalry force numbering around 1000 in the near vicinity. A brief skirmish then ensued, resulting in a number of Persian prisoners taken and leading to reports that not far off, an enormous army awaited battle with the Macedonians. Accordingly, Alexander rested his men, and constructed fortifications for his baggage camp. Four days later his army was on the move. As the full force of Darius' army came into view, Alexander halted his men and conducted a detailed reconnaissance to get the lay of the land and a better knowledge of the disposition and composition of the Persian Forces. After performing the reconnaissance of the enemy, Alexander then convened a council of Macedonian generals to determine the most efficacious course of action. General Parmenio, his most seasoned officer, recommended that the army launch a surprise night attack due to Darius' overwhelming troop strength. However, Alexander dismissed the plan as being only ordinary and lacking in audacity and exclaimed, "I will not steal victory like a thief." Alexander ultimately proved correct in his belief, since Darius anticipated a nighttime assault and kept his men awake throughout the entire night in anticipation.

On 1 October 331 BC, despite the prospects of facing one million Persian troops, Alexander, who apparently possessed no anxiety and who was supremely confident of victory, had to be roused numerous times in the morning by his general staff before waking and launching his attack.

Darius responded by launching his chariots on terrain that the Persians had meticulously smoothed over to ensure unimpeded swift movement to cut down the Macedonians. However, the Greeks countered this threat with javelin throwers along with a new tactic wherein the front ranks stepped aside to open a gap to permit the enemy chariots to partially penetrate their formation and then immediately close ranks with the rear formation and its 13-20 foot-long sarissas/pikes abruptly stopping the charioteers' advance since the horses feared charging into the pikes head-on. The charioteers, who were then cut off from the main body, were killed at the Macedonians' leisure.

Alexander, exploiting the speed and discipline of his companion cavalry, struck at the heart of the Persians and relentlessly pursued

Darius at the center of the formation. Darius, taken aback by the Greeks' audacious attack, fled the battlefield and the Persians retreated in panic. As with most ancient battles, the report of casualties varies, but some historians reported that the Persian losses may have been as high as 47,000 while the Macedonians suffered 4,000.

MAXIM #13

IF YOU'RE SHORT OF EVERYTHING BUT THE ENEMY, YOU'RE IN A COMBAT ZONE

Battle of Teutoburg Forest painted by Otto Albert Koch – (1897–1945)

Over four days at the beginning of September 9 AD, half of Rome's Western Army, consisting of the XVII, XVIII and XIX legions and commanded by Sextus Quinctilus Varus was ambushed in the German Teutoburg Forest and annihilated by forces commanded by Arminius (a German noble who was raised in Rome and who was serving as an Auxiliary in Rome's vaunted army in order to better learn Roman military tactics with the purpose of using this knowledge to one day defeat their German oppressor).

The battle began with the Roman army marching west into the Teutoburg Forest. Descriptions have the Roman force stretched out as much as nine miles in a narrow column. This seems logical since axe men would have been cutting down trees and the resulting roadway would have been narrow. When the army reached a point northeast of Osnabruck, they were ambushed. The historian Dio states that Arminius, while riding with Varus, asked to be excused to check on his auxiliaries but instead met up with the Germans to set up the attack.

Arminius then waited to launch his ambush in the midst of a heavy rainstorm while the Roman Legions were too far extended in column formation. Utterly taken by surprise, the Romans suffered significant casualties since they could not adequately deploy their forces in the forest while being targeted by German archers. However, by the end of the first day, the Romans had managed to regain their footing and build a fortified camp where they spent the first night. Assailed again in the morning, they were able to break out to the southeast and reached a point north of the Wiehen Hills and northwest of Ostercappeln. The following day the army resumed its trek to the northwest, still in heavy rain, arriving at an area north of the Kalkriese Hill, where the final massacre took place. Trapped in the narrow corridor between the Kalkriese Hill and the Great Bog, the rest of the army was destroyed.

In terms of the battle's aftermath, three Roman legions, three cavalry units and six auxiliary regiments consisting of 25,000 men were slaughtered and Varus, not wanting to be taken as prisoner and disgraced by his ignominious defeat, chose to commit suicide. After hearing of the annihilation of Rome's Western Army, the seventy-two-year-old Caesar Augustus screamed for Varus to "return his coveted captured eagles." In closing, this battle dealt a severe blow to the Roman Empire's imperial pretensions and was, along with the Battle of Cannae, one of Rome's greatest military defeats. As such, Rome's expansion in northern Europe was checked and it therefore was compelled to aggressively patrol the Rhineland borders in the hopes of preventing any future uprisings from Germania.

MAXIM #13

IF YOU'RE SHORT OF EVERYTHING BUT THE ENEMY, YOU'RE IN A COMBAT ZONE

Photos of the WWII, Battle of Stalingrad

The German offensive to capture Stalingrad began on August 23, 1942, using the 6th Army and elements of the 4th Panzer Army. The attack was supported by intensive *Luftwaffe* bombing that reduced much of the city to rubble. The fighting degenerated into house-to-house fighting; both sides poured reinforcements into the city. By mid-November 1942, the Germans had pushed the Soviet defenders back at great cost into narrow zones along the west bank of the Volga River.

On 19 November, 1942, the Red Army launched Operation *Uranus*, a two-pronged attack targeting the weaker Romanian and Hungarian armies protecting the German 6th Army's flanks. The Axis forces on the flanks were overrun and the 6th Army was cut off and surrounded in the Stalingrad area. Adolf Hitler ordered that the army stay in Stalingrad and make no attempt to break out; instead, attempts were made to supply the army by air and to break the encirclement from the outside. Heavy fighting continued for another two months. By the beginning of February 1943, the Axis forces in Stalingrad had exhausted their ammunition and food. The remaining units of the 6th Army surrendered on February 2, 1943.

The battle of Stalingrad is generally considered one of the decisive victories that led to the defeat of Nazi Germany and is commonly nicknamed as the bloodiest battle of WWII with an estimated 2 million casualties.

MAXIM #13

IF YOU'RE SHORT OF EVERYTHING BUT THE ENEMY, YOU'RE IN A COMBAT ZONE

A Painting of Napoleon III having a conversation with Bismarck after being captured in the Battle of Sedan (1878 painting by Wilhelm Camphausen)

The **Battle of Sedan** was fought during the Franco-Prussian War from 1 to 2 September 1870. It resulted in the capture of Emperor Napoleon III and large numbers of his troops and for all intents and purposes decided the war in favor of Prussia and its allies, though fighting continued under a new French government.

The battle opened with the French *Army of Châlons* commanded by Marshal Mac Mahon and consisting of 130,000 soldiers, 202 French infantry battalions, 80 cavalry squadrons and 564 guns, attacking the surrounding Prussian Third and Meuse Armies commanded by General Helmuth von Moltke and consisting of 200,000 soldiers that totaled 222 infantry battalions, 186 cavalry squadrons, and 774 guns.

Despite valiant repeated efforts to break out of the encirclement, the German artillery continued to mercilessly pound away at the beleaguered French forces. By the end of the day on September 1, Napoleon III called off the attacks and, with no hope of success, surrendered the following day. The French lost over 17,000 men killed and wounded with 21,000 captured while the Prussians reported their losses at only 2,320 killed, 5,980 wounded and 700 captured or missing.

The defeat at Sedan and the capture of Napoleon III and France's second line army, with the first-line French army being shut up in Metz, ultimately sealed the doom of France and thus decided the outcome of the war in Prussia's favor. With the Second Empire now overthrown, Napoleon III was permitted to leave Prussian custody for exile in England, while, within a fortnight, the Prussian Meuse Army and Third Army went on to besiege Paris.

MAXIM #13

IF YOU'RE SHORT OF EVERYTHING BUT THE ENEMY, YOU'RE IN A COMBAT ZONE

The **Battle of Tannenberg** was fought between Russia and Germany from August 26 to 30, 1914, during the first month of World War I. The battle resulted in the almost complete destruction of the Russian Second Army and the suicide of its commanding general, Alexander Samsonov. A series of follow-up battles (First Masurian Lakes) destroyed most of the First Army as well and kept the Russians off balance until the spring of 1915. The battle is particularly notable for fast rail movements by the Germans, enabling them to concentrate against each of the two Russian armies in turn, and for the failure of the Russians to encode their radio messages. It brought high prestige to both Field Marshal Paul von Hindenburg and his rising general staff-officer Erich Ludendorff.

Photo of the WWI Russian prisoners of war from Tannenberg, 1914

MAXIM #13

LESSON LEARNED

An operation without a "*Schwerpunkt*" (center of gravity) is like a man without character." – Field Marshal Paul von Hindenburg "If your enemy is secure at all points, be prepared for him. If he is in superior strength, evade him. If your opponent is temperamental, seek to irritate him. Pretend to be weak, that he may grow arrogant. If he is taking his ease, give him no rest. If his forces are united, separate them. Attack him where he is unprepared, appear where you are not expected." – Sun Tzu, The Art of War Do not get involved in a battle of attrition. Rather, ensure that your military objective emphasizes the use of an "economy of force."

*Waterloo Gordons and Greys to the Front,
Painting by Stanley Berkeley – (1855–1909)*

MAXIM #14

THE ONLY THING MORE DANGEROUS TO YOU THAN THE ENEMY IS YOUR ALLIES

The Duke of Wellington at Waterloo,
Painting by Robert Alexander Hillingford – (1828–1904)

"As Lord Chesterfield said of the Generals of his day, I only hope that when the enemy reads the list of their names, he trembles as I do." – Duke of Wellington.

Stalin's purge of the Red Army officer corps during the 1930s (consisting of three of five marshals equivalent to five-star generals, 13 of 15 army commanders equivalent to three- and four-star generals, eight of nine admirals, 50 of 57 corps commanders equivalent to three-star generals, 154 of 186 division commanders equivalent to two-star generals, 16 of 16 army commissars and 25 of 28 army corps commissars) left him an army full of incompetent generals afraid to be too successful lest they be perceived as a threat. Nazi Germany, aware that the Russian army's senior

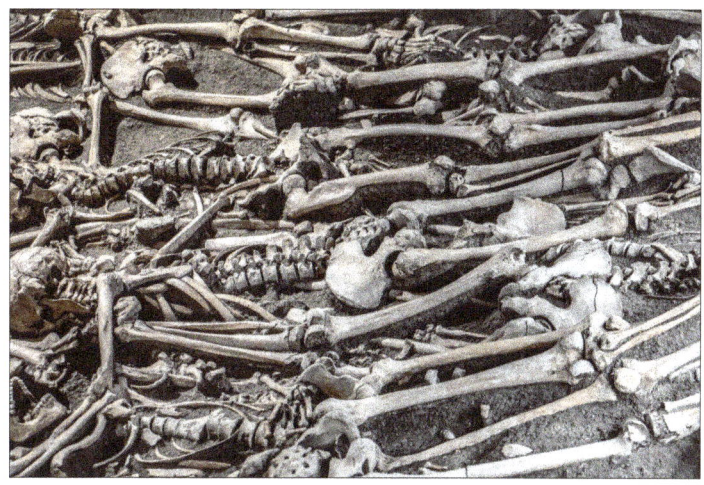

Photo of a mass grave – victims of Stalin's Great Purge

officer ranks were severely depleted, exploited this weakness and decided to invade the Soviet Union on September 22, 1941 under the codename "Operation Barbarossa," which would ultimately claim the lives of over 18 million Russians. Had Stalin not decimated his officer ranks and killed millions during his purge to consolidate power, it is likely that Germany would have thought twice about invading.

MAXIM #14

LESSON LEARNED

When selecting allies to aggregate military capabilities and provide legitimacy for the use of force in protecting US strategic interests that are committed to combatting countries that threaten the Global Order, it is important to choose competent allies who are willing to endure the same sacrifices required to effectively quell violent extremists, nuclear rogue nation states, narco-terrorists, cyber criminals and revisionist authoritarian powers.

General Washington and Lafayette Shaking Hands

British Newspaper Illustration of East meets West, 1905

MAXIM #15

A RETREATING ARMY IS PROBABLY JUST FALLING BACK AND REGROUPING

Last Stand of King Harold at the Battle of Hastings on 14th October 1066 in the Norman Invasion

English King Harold Godwinson II formed his infantry into a shield-wall along an opportune defensive position atop a hill. Forced to charge uphill into awaiting spears, swords, and axes, Norman King William the Conqueror's cavalry failed to penetrate the line. Whether in retreat or perhaps a feigned retreat (it's debated and will never be resolved), the Norman cavalry fell back, and the engaging wing of Harold's army followed, breaking the unity of the line. In counterattack, William's forces first struck their disorganized pursuers and then turned on the weakened flank of the shield-wall.

William Poitiers writes: "The Normans and their allies observing that they could not overcome an enemy which was so numerous and so solidly drawn up without severe losses, retreated, simulating flight as a trick…among the barbarians there was great joy…some thousands of them…threw themselves in pursuit of those whom they believed to be in flight. Suddenly, the Normans reigned in their horses, intercepted and surrounded (the enemy) and killed them to the last man."

William of Malmesbury provides a similar account: "The English formed an impenetrable body, which could have kept them safe that day, if the Normans had not tricked them into opening their ranks by a feigned flight."

MAXIM #15

A RETREATING ARMY IS PROBABLY JUST FALLING BACK AND REGROUPING

*"The Battle of Austerlitz 1805" painted in 1810
by Baron François Pascal Simon Gerard (1770–1837)*

The Battle of Austerlitz, which occurred on December 2, 1805, was the climactic battle of the War of the Third Coalition (August – December 1805). Having forced an Austrian army to surrender at Ulm in September, Napoleon then chased the Russian army of Mikhail Ilarionovich Kutuzov from the Austrian border on the River Inn to Moravia. There Kutuzov's army linked up with reinforcements from Russia and Tsar Alexander I joined his troops. Also known as the Battle of the Three Emperors, because Napoleon, Emperor Franz of Austria, and Alexander I were all present on the field, Austerlitz was a crushing French victory that sealed the fate of the Third Coalition (Russia, Austria, Great Britain, Naples, and Sweden).

Napoleon's forces were inferior to those of the coalition, so the French emperor developed a ruse. Having initially seized the dominant Pratzen Heights in the middle of the battlefield, he withdrew from that position, feigning weakness, in order to entice the allies to attack his right flank. When they did so, Napoleon's forces retook the Pratzen Heights, where Kutuzov and Alexander himself urged their troops to resist, and then surrounded the remnants of the allied army, inflicting approximately 30 percent casualties on the Russian and Austrian troops.

The victory was so one-sided that Alexander withdrew his army from the campaign altogether, retreating rapidly back to Russian Poland. His departure compelled Emperor Franz to sue for peace, resulting in the lopsided Treaty of Pressburg (1806), which formally ended the war and dissolved the coalition. Although little studied by Russians and Austrians (for reasons of national pride), Austerlitz elsewhere became the paradigm of decisive battles in the nineteenth century, and generals across the continent and even in the United States sought to emulate Napoleon's accomplishment.

MAXIM #15

A RETREATING ARMY IS PROBABLY JUST FALLING BACK AND REGROUPING

Photo representation of French soldiers in action at the Battle of Verdun, WWI, 1916

Verdun, 1916. After the Battle of the Marne in 1914, when the Kaiser's armies failed to defeat France, the Germans stood on the defensive in the west while they attacked in the east. Only once, until 1918, did they deviate from this strategy – at the beginning of 1916. The Chief of the German General Staff, Erich von Falkenhayn, a withdrawn, unpopular figure with a curious mix of ruthlessness and indecision, came up with a novel concept in the history of warfare.

Instead of trying to defeat the French outright, he would bait them into defending a point in the line it could not afford to abandon. There he would "bleed it white," the very terminology of a war which, more than any other, treated soldiers' lives as little more than corpuscles.

He selected Verdun, rated the world's strongest fortress, with a centuries-long tradition in *la défense de France*, and only 150 miles east of Paris. The 1914 campaign had left it in a narrow salient, vulnerable on three sides to overwhelming German superiority in heavy artillery.

On the 21st of February, 1,220 German guns opened up on a frontage of barely 8 miles, launching the most savage artillery barrage in history. The French lines sagged but held, at tremendous cost. The immortal slogan "They shall not pass" was coined. In what became an affair of national honor, France rose to the bait. For ten hideous months, history's longest battle raged.

The tragic irony was that Verdun bled the attacking Germans almost equally. What began as a small affair resulted in combined casualties of over 800,000 men – most of them inflicted in an area not much bigger than New York's Central Park.

Verdun cost Germany her last chance at defeating the Allies in the West, but the impact on France, elevating the defeatist Marshal Pétain as its hero, went far deeper. French losses led to the demoralization that defeated her in 1940. The Pyrrhic victory *par excellence*, Verdun was a murderous blunder for both sides.

MAXIM #15
LESSON LEARNED

A feigned retreat is a military tactic whereby a military force pretends to withdraw or to have been routed, in order to lure an enemy into a position of vulnerability.

A feigned retreat is one of the more difficult tactics for a military force to undertake and requires well-disciplined soldiers. This is because if the enemy presses into the retreating body,

Painting –Retreat Scene from the Russian-French War, 1812 by Bogdan Willewalde – (1818–1903)

undisciplined troops are likely to lose coherence and the rout will become genuine.

Sun Tzu, in the Chinese military treatise *The Art of War*, writes: "Do not pursue an enemy who simulates flight." This advice cautions against pursuing an enemy that unexpectedly runs away or shows a weaker force, as it may be bait for an ambush.

As such, don't swallow the bait and remain vigilant and vigorously execute continual reconnaissance.

MAXIM #16

DON'T LOOK CONSPICUOUS; IT DRAWS FIRE!

Rough Riders at San Juan Heights, Santiago, Cuba 1898, National Archives, Washington, D.C.

Theodore Roosevelt writes in his book entitled "The Battles for Kettle and San Juan Hills" that Captain Bucky O'Neill (an officer who subscribed to the combat maxim that an officer should never take cover) was strolling up and down in front of his men, smoking his cigarette whereupon his men begged him to lie down. One of his sergeants exclaimed, "Captain, a bullet is sure to hit you." O'Neill then took his cigarette out of his mouth and, blowing out a cloud of smoke laughed and said, "Sergeant, there isn't a Spanish bullet made that will kill me." Moments later, while discussing with a fellow officer from which direction the Spanish fire was coming, he was struck in the mouth and the bullet exited out the back of his head.

MAXIM #16
DON'T LOOK CONSPICUOUS; IT DRAWS FIRE!

Major Richthofen and his famous Fokker DR-1

Manfred Albrecht Freiherr von Richthofen (May 2, 1892– April 21,1918), also widely known as the **Red Baron**, was a German fighter pilot with the Imperial German Army Air Service (*Luftstreitkräfte*) during World War I. He is considered the top ace of that war, being officially credited with 80 air combat victories.

Originally a cavalryman, Richthofen transferred to the Air Service in 1915, becoming one of the first members of *Jasta 2* in 1916. He quickly distinguished himself as a fighter pilot, and during 1917 became leader of *Jasta 11* and then the larger unit *Jagdgeschwader 1* (better known as the "Flying Circus"). By 1918, he was regarded as a national hero in Germany, and was very well known and respected by his enemy.

Richthofen, while flying his easily recognizable red Fokker DR-1 triplane, was shot down and killed near Amiens on April 21, 1918. He reportedly was discovered sitting upright in his seat with his thumb depressed on the machine gun trigger mechanism. He was buried by the Allied forces with full military honors.

World War I aircraft in dogfight

MAXIM #16

DON'T LOOK CONSPICUOUS; IT DRAWS FIRE!

Cannon targeting the sea at the Rock of Gibraltar

The Siege of Gibraltar of 1727 (thirteenth siege of Gibraltar, second by Spain) saw Spanish forces besiege the British garrison of Gibraltar as part of the Anglo-Spanish War. Depending on the sources, Spanish troops numbered between 12,000 and 25,000. British defenders were 1,500 at the beginning of the siege, increasing up to about 5,000. After a five-month siege with several unsuccessful and costly assaults, Spanish troops gave up and withdrew. Following the failure, the war drew to a close, opening the way for the 1728 Treaty of El Pardo and the Treaty of Seville signed in 1729.

Excerpt from the diary of a British soldier in the garrison of Gibraltar: March 9th: 'Came a deserter who reports that while our guns were firing at them an officer pulled off his hat, huzzaed and called God to damn us all, when one of our balls with unerring justice took off the miserable man's head and left him a wretched example of the Divine Justice.'

MAXIM #16

LESSON LEARNED

Employ effective cover and concealment techniques in order to survive the battlefield and successfully execute your mission. As an age-old Japanese adage warns, the nail that sticks up the most is the first one to be hit.

Photo of U.S. sniper employing an effective concealment technique

MAXIM #17
LIGHT INFANTRY ISN'T LIGHT

Photo of U.S. Airborne Infantrymen

MAXIM #17

LIGHT INFANTRY ISN'T LIGHT

Roman Legionary Soldier British Infantry, Revolutionary War, 1776

Roman infantrymen in General Marius' army, circa 100 BC, carried armor, weapons and 15 days' rations approximating 60–80 pounds. To ease their burden, Marius issued each legionary a cross stick to carry their loads on their shoulders and, as such, the soldiers were nicknamed *Marius' Mules* because of the amount of gear they had to carry themselves. British soldiers in 1776, in similar fashion, carried comparable combat loads.

Fully equipped US soldier patrolling in Eastern Afghanistan during operation Enduring Freedom, 2011

The 2003 U.S. CALL Task Force Devil Combined Arms Assessment Team report found the average fighting load for an infantry platoon member to be between 62.43 and 81.38 pounds, depending on position. Paratroopers and Special Operations forces have even carried loads in excess of 120 pounds. The emergency approach march load fell between 127.35 and 147.82 pounds. These measurements were taken by weighing absolutely everything troops carried with them, including water. These figures are in line with the history of soldier load carriage.

MAXIM #17

LESSON LEARNED

During the Afghanistan War, a senior British army officer commented that the Taliban refer to British soldiers as "donkeys" who move in a tactical "waddle" because of the weight they carried, which averaged 110 pounds. The officer further elaborated by stating that "our infantry finds it almost impossible to close with the enemy because the bad guys are twice as mobile."

So, the million-dollar question is, what should a combat load weigh or how much should a soldier carry?

The Marine Corps Combat Development Command's 2003 Combat Load Report cites S.L.A. Marshall's book "The *Soldier's Load and the Mobility of a Nation*" as the premier source on the subject. Marshall concludes that a soldier could optimally carry 33 percent of his body weight. The same Marine Corps study determined the average weight of a Marine male was 169 pounds and the average female was 130 pounds. This would put their combat loads at 56 pounds and 42 pounds, respectively.

The Army field manual on foot marches, **FM 21–18**, which has not been updated since 1990, does not consider individual body weight. It prescribes a fighting load of no more than 48 pounds and an approach march load of 72 pounds. There is, however, a caveat to those weights. The manual states, "The primary consideration is not how much a soldier can carry, but how much he can carry without impaired combat effectiveness—mentally or physically." This essentially bases a determination about the amount carried on individual capabilities.

US Infantry paratrooper toting a machine-gun

MAXIM #18

Body Count Math – 3 Guerrillas + 1 probable + 2 pigs = 37 enemies killed in action

A military **body count** is simply the total number of confirmed kills in battle that enables commanders to better evaluate the efficacy of a mission and to ultimately determine how best to allocate future resources and manpower to accomplish the strategic objective to vanquish the enemy.

Sassanian Empire. According to Procopius, when the Persians are about to march to a war, the king sits on the throne and many baskets are set before him. The men of the army pass along the baskets one by one, each throwing one arrow in the baskets, which are then sealed with the king's seal. When the army returns to Persia, each man takes an arrow, and the number of casualties will be determined by the number of remaining arrows.

Ancient Persian archer statue in the Niavaran Palace Complex Garden, Tehran, Iran

Vietnam War – *Main article: Vietnam War body count controversy*
Since the goal of the United States in the Vietnam War was not to conquer North Vietnam but rather to ensure the survival of the South Vietnamese government, measuring progress was difficult. All the contested territory was theoretically "held" already. Instead, the US Army used body counts to show that the US was winning the war. The Army's theory was that eventually, the Vietcong and North Vietnamese Army would lose after the attrition warfare.

According to historian Christian Appy, "search and destroy was the principal tactic; and the enemy body count was the primary measure of progress" in General Westmoreland's war of attrition. Search and destroy was coined as a phrase in 1965 to describe missions aimed at flushing the Viet Cong out of hiding, while the body count was the measuring stick for the success of any operation.

Photo of a U.S. Army Forward Operations Base during the Vietnam War

MAXIM #18
LESSON LEARNED

It is still true, as the great Prussian military theorist Karl von Clausewitz noted more than 160 years ago, that "casualty reports ... are never accurate" and, in any case, such figures are "no accurate measure of the loss of morale; hence ... the abandonment of the fight remains the only authentic proof of victory."

General H. Norman Schwarzkopf, the allied commander for Desert Storm in the Persian Gulf War of January 1991, has emphatically stated that as a Vietnam veteran he abhors body counts as a measure of military success, and that he thinks such statistics are not only meaningless but misleading and that body counts can push junior commanders into a numbers game that compromises their integrity. He later vowed in his press conferences that the U.S. Central Command will never engage in the body-count business.

Iraq War – *Main article: Casualties of the Iraq War*

During the 2003 invasion of Iraq, following General Schwarzkopf's lead, the US military adopted an official policy of not counting deaths. General Tommy Franks' statement that "we don't do body counts" was widely reported. Critics claimed that Franks was only attempting to evade bad publicity, while supporters pointed to the failure of body counts to give an accurate impression of the state of the war in Vietnam. At the end of October 2005, it became public that the US military had been counting Iraqi fatalities since January 2004 but only those killed by insurgents and not those killed by the US forces.

Number of Deaths	
Source: Iraq Body Count Report–The Guardian Iraq Body Count 2003–2011	114,212
Iraq War Logs – New Civilian & Comparable Host Nation Remaining Central Estimate	13,750
Iraq War Logs – Host Nation Combatant – Central Estimate	5,575
Iraq War Logs – Enemy (minus IBC overlaps) – Central Estimate	20,499
Insurgents Killed June–December 2003	597
Insurgents Killed May 2004	652
Insurgents and Iraqi Soldiers Killed March 2009	59
Insurgents and Iraqi Soldiers Killed 2010–2011	2,187
TOTAL IRAQI	157,531
US & Coalition Military Killed 2003–2011	4,802
TOTAL	**162,333**

MAXIM #19

IF YOUR POSITIONS ARE FIRMLY SET AND YOU ARE PREPARED TO TAKE THE ENEMY ASSAULT ON, HE WILL BYPASS YOU OR FORTIFY YOUR FRONT AND YOU'LL GET YOUR REAR SHOT UP

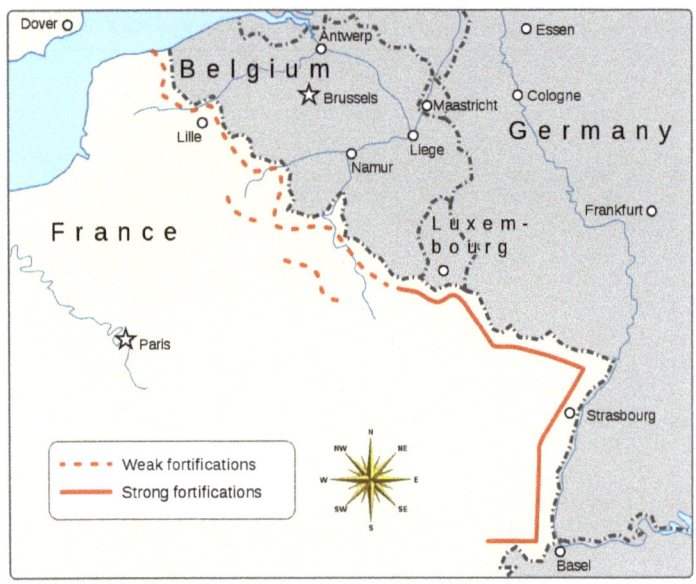

Photo of a bunker at Alsace, France and the Maginot Line location

The **Maginot Line**, named after the French Minister of War André Maginot, was a line of concrete fortifications, obstacles, and weapon installations built by France in the 1930s to deter invasion by Germany and force them to move around the fortifications. Constructed on the French side of its borders with Italy, Switzerland, Germany, and Luxembourg, the line did not extend to the English Channel due to French strategy that envisioned a move into Belgium to counter a German assault.

Based on France's experience with trench warfare during World War I, the massive Maginot Line was built in the run-up to World War II, after the Locarno Conference gave rise to a fanciful and optimistic "Locarno spirit." French military experts extolled the Line as a work of genius that would deter German aggression, because it would slow an invasion force long enough for French forces to mobilize and counterattack. The Maginot Line was impervious to most forms of attack, including aerial bombings and tank fire, and had underground railways as a backup; it also had state-of-the-art living conditions for garrisoned troops, supplying air conditioning and eating areas for their comfort. Instead of attacking directly, the Germans invaded through the Low Countries, bypassing the Line to the north. French and British officers had anticipated this: when Germany invaded the Netherlands and Belgium, they carried out plans to form an aggressive front that cut across Belgium and connected to the Maginot Line. However, the French line was weak near the Ardennes forest. The French believed this region, with its rough terrain, would be an unlikely invasion route of German forces; if it was traversed, it would be done at a slow rate that would allow the French time to bring up reserves and counterattack. The German army, having reformulated their plans from a repeat of the First World War-era plan, became aware of and exploited this weak point in the French defensive front. A rapid advance through the forest and across the River Meuse encircled much of the Allied forces, resulting in a sizeable force being evacuated at Dunkirk leaving the forces to the south unable to mount an effective resistance to the German invasion of France. The line has since become a metaphor for expensive efforts that offer a false sense of security.

MAXIM #19

IF YOUR POSITIONS ARE FIRMLY SET AND YOU ARE PREPARED TO TAKE THE ENEMY ASSAULT ON, HE WILL BYPASS YOU OR FORTIFY YOUR FRONT AND YOU'LL GET YOUR REAR SHOT UP

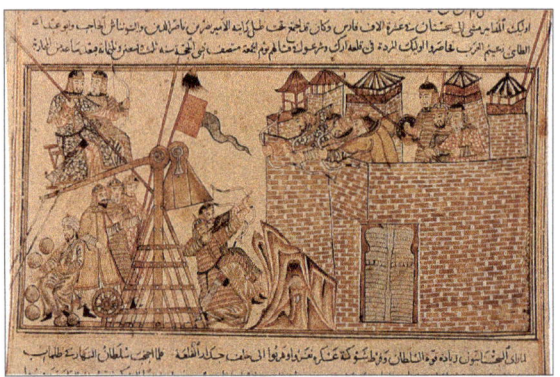

Genghis Khan's siege of the Great Wall of China

The **history of the Great Wall of China** began when fortifications built by various states during the Spring and Autumn (771–476 BC) and Warring States periods (475–221 BC) were connected by the first emperor of China, Qin Shi Huang, to protect his newly founded Qin dynasty (221–206 BC) against incursions by nomads from Inner Asia. The walls were built of rammed earth, constructed using forced labor, and by 212 BC ran from Gansu to the coast of southern Manchuria.

In the 13th century, the Mongol leader Genghis Khan, once a vassal of the Jurchens, rose up against the Jin dynasty. In the ensuing Mongol conquest of the Jin dynasty, the nomadic invaders avoided direct attacks on the Jin fortifications. Instead, when they could, the Mongols simply rode around the walls; an effective example of this tactic is in 1211, when they circumvented the substantial fortress in Zhangjiakou and inflicted a terrible defeat upon the Jin armies at the Battle of Yehuling. The Mongols also took advantage of lingering Liao resentment against the Jin; the Khitan defenders of the garrisons along the Jin walls, such as those in Gubeikou, often preferred to surrender to the Mongols rather than fight them. The only major engagement of note along the main Great Wall line was at the heavily defended Juyong Pass: instead of laying siege, the Mongol general Jebe lured the defenders out into an ambush and charged in through the opened gates. In 1215, Genghis Khan besieged, captured, and sacked the Jin capital of Yanjing (modern-day Beijing). The Jin dynasty eventually collapsed following the siege of Caizhou in 1234. Western Xia had already fallen in 1227, and the Southern Song resisted the Mongols until 1279.

Why did Genghis Khan's breach of the Great Wall prove successful while others failed?
- He spent five years making thorough preparations for his battle against the Jin Court and realized that to breach the Great Wall, he needed to keep the Jin off-balance by attacking weaker areas first.
- He defeated the Western Xia to its west, which was an "assistant" to Jin but a threat to the Mongols.
- He defeated the enemies to his north to ensure the safety of his territory.
- He recruited the Jin army which guarded the northwest section of the Jin Great Wall, making the area a military base for attacking the Jin.
- He subverted the Jin garrison soldiers for his use.
- He collected information on the Jin court from merchants, envoys and spies.
- The Jin emperor did not take the Mongols seriously at first and put most of his military forces on the southern border with Southern Song (1127–1279 AD). Also, having fallen into disrepair in many parts, the Great Wall at that time was not as solid as it used to be.

MAXIM #19

LESSON LEARNED

"If we wish to fight, the enemy can be forced to an engagement even though he be sheltered behind a high rampart and a deep ditch. All we need do is attack some other place that he will be obliged to relieve. So, in war, the way is to avoid what is strong and to strike at what is weak." – Sun Tzu, **Art of War**.

A WWI German Infantry Captain named Willy Rohr was one of the first officers who implemented the "Stormtrooper" doctrine that emphasized the following infiltration tactics in dealing with strongpoints:

Photo of WWI German Stormtroopers in action

- Use decentralized, small units, rather than large ones, to bypass strongpoints in the enemy line.
- Attack and cripple nerve centers and other "soft" (vulnerable) targets and strike hard and fast and keep on moving. Aim in the first wave to disrupt and paralyze, rather than to destroy and occupy ground. Let future waves of infantry mop up the rest.
- **Use "mission orders."** Mission orders are orders in which a commander states his objectives and goals, rather than a detailed description of how something should be done. In simple terms, mission orders tell someone what to do and let him decide how to do it. This frees up the small unit leader to use his own initiative and creativity. It gets rid of micromanagement at the unit level and increases the tempo of operations, since leaders do not need to check with their superiors before doing everything.
- **Rely on initiative.** Promote and rely on those who show initiative, and disfavor those who do not. The only way to overcome the confusion and disorder of battle is to have men who can use their own initiative on the spot to make decisions. Making decisions and carrying them out faster than the enemy will jump-start operational tempo and will keep the enemy permanently off-balance.
- **Use different equipment that is better suited to the job**. Rohr liked weapons that focused on speed and maneuver. He emphasized grenades, shorter rifles or portable automatic weapons, flamethrowers, and light mortars. The trooper should move quickly in small squads, destroying critical obstacles, and keep moving forward.

MAXIM #20
IF YOU ARE FORWARD OF YOUR POSITION, YOUR ARTILLERY WILL FALL SHORT

Artillery Barrage

WWI Photo British gunners in action with an 18 LB Gun

On the night of 4–5 August 1916, during the First Battle of the Somme, the 13th Battalion of the Durham Light Infantry was fired on by Australian artillery while in process of capturing and holding on to a German communication trench called Munster Alley.

October 4, 1918 – The nine companies from the US Army's 77th Infantry Division which had pushed into a salient at Charlevaux, France and became known as the "Lost Battalion" after being surrounded by the Germans, were subjected to friendly artillery fire for several hours, either due to the artillery fire being inaccurate or the coordinates, delivered by carrier pigeon, being inaccurate. The overall commander, Major Charles Whittlesey, used his last carrier pigeon, named Cher Ami, to send a second message for the artillery to cease fire.

MAXIM #20

IF YOU ARE FORWARD OF YOUR POSITION, YOUR ARTILLERY WILL FALL SHORT

U.S. Army Sherman Tank WWII

Operation Cobra was the codename for an offensive launched by the First United States Army and commanded by Lieutenant General Omar Bradley during the Normandy Campaign of World War II. The intent of the mission was to take advantage of the distraction of the Germans by the British and Canadian attacks around Caen in Operation Goodwood and break through the German defenses that were penning in his troops, while the Germans were unbalanced. Once a corridor had been created, the First Army would then be able to advance into Brittany, rolling up the German flanks once free of the constraints of the bocage country.

On July 25, 1944, 600 Allied fighter bombers attacked strongpoints and enemy artillery along a 300-yard wide strip of ground by the St. Lo area. During the following hour, 1800 heavy bombers from the U.S. 8th Air Force saturated a 6,000-yard x 2,200-yard area of the St. Lo-Periers road, which was then followed by a final wave of medium bombers.

General Bradley specifically requested that the bombers approach the target from the east, out of the sun and parallel to the St. Lo-Periers road in order to minimize the risk of friendly losses but most of the airmen instead came in from the north perpendicular to the front line since the heavy bomber commanders felt that a parallel approach was impossible due to the time and space constraints that Bradley had set. Moreover, a parallel approach would not have assured that all the bombs would fall behind Germany lines because of deflection errors or obscured aiming points due to smoke and dust.

Thus, despite US ground forces' attempt to identify their positions to 8th Army Air Force personnel, 111 Americans were killed and 490 wounded, including General Bradley's friend and fellow West Pointer, Lieutenant General Lesley McNair, the highest-ranking U.S. soldier to be killed in action in the European Theater of Operations.

MAXIM #20

LESSON LEARNED

Identify and assess potential fratricide risks in the estimate of the situation. Express these risks in the Operations Order (OPORD) and/or applicable Fragmentary Orders (FRAGOs).

Maintain situational awareness. Focus on such areas as current intelligence, unit locations/dispositions, denial areas (minefields/scatterable mines), and contaminated areas, such as ICM and NBC; SITREPs; and METT-TC factors.

Ensure positive target identification. Review vehicle and weapons identification (ID) cards. Become familiar with the characteristics of potential friendly and enemy vehicles, including their silhouettes and thermal signatures. Know at what ranges and under what conditions positive identification of various vehicles and weapons is possible. (**NOTE:** Refer to the special note at the start of this section.)

Maintain effective fire control. Ensure fire commands are accurate, concise, and clearly stated. Make it mandatory for crewmen to ask for clarification of any portion of the fire command that they do not completely understand. Stress the importance of the chain of command in the fire control process; ensure crewmen get in the habit of obtaining target confirmation and permission to fire from their leaders before engaging targets they assume are enemy elements.

Establish a command climate that emphasizes fratricide prevention. Enforce fratricide prevention measures, placing special emphasis on the use of doctrinally sound TTP. Ensure constant supervision in the execution of orders and in the performance of all tasks and missions to standard.

Photo of Russian artillery in action

MAXIM #21

THE MOST DANGEROUS THING ON THE BATTLEFIELD IS A 2ND LIEUTENANT EQUIPPED WITH A MAP AND COMPASS

U.S. Army lensatic compass with topographic map

The ability to navigate terrain with a map and compass is a skill set that has become lost in recent years due to technological advances like GPS and its integration into our smartphones. For many of us, navigating a city without a GPS would simply seem ridiculous. In effect, many soldiers have become so used to the integration of our "devices" into everyday life that they have lost their ability to perform a simple task, like leaving point A and arriving at point B without external help. During Operation Iraqi Freedom in 2005, a U.S. junior infantry officer's convoy encountered sand-storm conditions that negatively affected the vehicle's Global Positioning System to precisely identify the unit's location. The lieutenant, who was lacking confidence in his map-reading skills, then flagged a taxi to escort the convoy back to the Forward Operating Base.

MAXIM #21

LESSON LEARNED

Cartography is the art and science of expressing the known physical features of the earth graphically by maps and charts. No one knows who drew, molded, laced together, or scratched out in the dirt the first map. But a study of history reveals that the most pressing demands for accuracy and detail in mapping have come as the result of military needs. Today, the complexities of tactical operations and deployment of troops are such that it is essential for all Soldiers to be able to read and interpret their maps in order to move quickly and effectively on the battlefield – U.S. Army Field Manual 3–25.26 Map Reading and Land Navigation (January 2005).

U.S. Army Land Navigation training photo

MAXIM #22

RECOILLESS RIFLES-AREN'T

Photo of US soldier firing a Recoilless Rifle

A **recoilless rifle** (RCLR) or **recoilless gun** is a type of lightweight tube artillery that is designed to allow some of the propellant gases to escape out the rear of the weapon at the moment of ignition, creating forward thrust that counteracts **<u>some</u>** of the weapon's recoil.

MAXIM #22

LESSON LEARNED

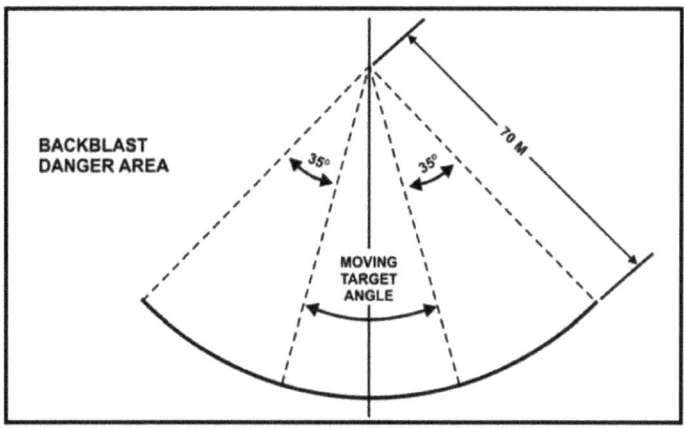

Figure 2-12. M72A4/A5/A6/A7 backblast area.

Backblast Diagram for the M72A4 Backblast Area Diagram, U.S. Army Field Manual

DANGER

WHEN OPERATING THE LIGHT ANTI TANK WEAPON (LAW) OR RECOILLESS RIFLE, KEEP IT POINTED DOWNRANGE. ENSURE YOUR WHOLE BODY IS CLEAR OF THE MUZZLE AND REAR OF THE LAUNCHER AND ENSURE THE BACKBLAST AREA IS CLEAR.

SUGGESTED READING LIST

Battle of Thermopylae – 480 BC
Cartledge, Paul (2006). *Thermopylae: The Battle That Changed the World*. Woodstock, New York: The Overlook Press. *ISBN 1-58567-566-0*.
Pressfield, Steven (1998). *Gates of Fire: An Epic Novel of the Battle of Thermopylae*. Doubleday. *ISBN 1407066595*.

Siege of Tyre – 332 BC
Jongeling, Hans, *The Siege of Tyre by Alexander the Great in 332 BC* (2008 Master Thesis). Archived from the original on 2011-08-05.

Battle of Gaugamela – 331 BC
Green, Peter (2013). *Alexander of Macedon, 356–323 BC: A Historical Biography*. Berkeley and Los Angeles, California: University of California Press. *ISBN 978-0-520-95469-4*.

Battle of Cannae – 216 BC
Lazenby, John Francis (1998) [1978]. *Hannibal's War: A Military History of the Second Punic War*. Wilts: University of Oklahoma Press. *ISBN 978-0806130040*.

Healy, Mark (1994). "Cannae: Hannibal Smashes Rome's Army". Sterling Heights: Osprey. *ISBN 978-1855324701*.

Battle of Alesia – 52 BC
Julius Caesar (ca. 45 BC), Commentaries on the Gallic Wars, Harvard University Press. *ISBN 0-674-99080-3*.

J.F.C. *Fuller*, Julius Caesar: Man, Soldier, and Tyrant, Da Capo Press, 1991, *ISBN 0-306-80422-0*

Battle at Teutoburg Forest – 9 AD
Creasy, E. S. (July 24, 2012). *The Fifteen Decisive Battles from Marathon to Waterloo*. Wildside Press LLC. ISBN 1434484424. Retrieved January 16, 2015.

Siege of Masada – 73 AD
Yadin, Yigael (1966). *Masada; Herod's fortress and the Zealot's last stand*. New York: Random House. OCLC 1175632

Battle of Hastings – 1066
Gravett, Christopher (1992). *Hastings 1066: The Fall of Saxon England*. Campaign. **13. Oxford, UK: Osprey.** ISBN 1-84176-133-8.

Battle of Jacob Ford – 1179
R.C. Smail, "Crusaders' Castles of the Twelfth Century", Cambridge Historical Journal 10, no. 2 (1951)

Battle of Hattin – 1187
Baldwin, M.W. (1936), Raymond III of Tripolis and the Fall of Jerusalem 91140-1187), Princeton: Princeton University Press

Brundage, James (1962), "De Expugnatione Terrae Sanctae per Saladinium" The Crusades: A Documentary Survey, Milwaukee: Marquette University Press

Siege of Acre – 1189
Hosler, John (2018). *The Siege of Acre, 1189–1191: Saladin, Richard the Lionheart, and the Battle that Decided the Third Crusade*. Yale University Press. ISBN 978-0-30021-550-2.

Mongolian Invasions of 1207, 1222 and 1287
Turnbull, Stephen (2003). *Genghis Khan and the Mongol Conquests 1190–1400* Oxford: Osprey Publishing. ISBN 978-1-84176-523-5

Siege of Rochester Castle – 1215
Turner, Ralph (2009). *King John: England's Evil King?* Stroud, UK: History Press. ISBN 978-0-7524-4850-3.

Stand of the Swiss Guard – 1527
Pitts, Vincent Joseph (1993). *The man who sacked Rome: Charles de Bourbon, constable of France (1490–1527)*. American university studies / 9, Series 9, History, Vol. 142. New York: P. Lang. ISBN 978-0-8204-2456-9.

Battle of Lützen – 1632
Weir, William (2004). *50 Battles That Changed the World: The Conflicts That Most Influenced the Course of History*. Savage, MD: Barnes & Noble. ISBN 0-7607-6609-6.

Battle of Salzbach-1675
Lynn, John (1996). *The Wars of Louis XIV, 1667-1714 (Modern Wars In Perspective)*. Longman. ISBN 978-0582056299.

Battle of Austerlitz – 1805, Battle of Moscow – 1812 and Battle of Waterloo – 1815
Chandler, David G. (1995). *The Campaigns of Napoleon*. New York: Simon & Schuster. ISBN 0-02-523660-1.

Goetz, Robert. *1805: Austerlitz: Napoleon and the Destruction of the Third Coalition* (Greenhill Books, 2005). ISBN 1-85367-644-6

Zamoyski, Adam. *Moscow 1812: Napoleon's Fatal March (Harper Collins, 2004)*. ISBN 0-06-107558-2

Siege of the Alamo – 1836
Tinkle, Lon (1985), *13 Days to Glory: The Siege of the Alamo*, College Station, TX: Texas A&M University Press, ISBN 0-89096-238-3. Reprint. Originally published: New York: McGraw-Hill, 1958

Charge of the Light Brigade, Crimean War – 1854

Terry Brighton. *(2004) Hell Riders: The True Story of the Charge of the Light Brigade*, Henry Holt and Co, ISBN 0-8050-7722-7.

Forgotten Heroes: The Charge of the Light Brigade, Roy Dutton, InfoDial Ltd., *ISBN 0-9556554-0-4*, published 25 October 2007.

Battles of Gettysburg and Chancellorsville – 1863

Catton, Bruce. Glory Road. Garden City, NY: Doubleday and Company, 1952. *ISBN 0-385-04167-5.*

Keegan, John. The American Civil War: A Military History. New York: Alfred A. Knopf, 2009. *ISBN 978-0-307-26343-8.*

Gallagher, Gary W. The Battle of Chancellorsville. National Park Service Civil War series. Conshohocken, PA: U.S. National Park Service and Eastern National, 1995. *ISBN 0-915992-87-6*

Battle of Camaron – 1863

Brunon, Jean (1981). *Camerone.* Paris: Editions France.

U.S. Indian Wars and Battle of Little Big Horn – 1876

Monnett, John H. (July 16, 2010), Where a Hundred Soldiers Were Killed: The Struggle for the Powder River Country in 1866 and the Making of the Fetterman Myth. University of New Mexico Press, *ISBN 978-0826345042.*

Robinson, Charles M. III (1995). A Good Year to Die: the story of the great Sioux war. New York: Random House. ISBN 0-679-43025-3.

Battle of Sedan–1870

Howard, M. (1961). The Franco-Prussian War: The German Invasion of France 1870–1871. London: Rupert Hart-Davis. ISBN 0-24663-587-8.

Zuber, Terence (2008). *The Moltke Myth: Prussian War Planning, 1857–1871.* Lanham, Maryland: University Press of America. ISBN 978-0761841616.

Battle of Saigo – 1877
Ravina, Mark. (2004). *The Last Samurai: The Life and Battles of Saigo Takamori.* Hoboken, New Jersey: Wiley. ISBN 9780471089704; OCLC 427566169

Battle of Rorke's Drift – 1879
Knight, Ian, *Rorke's Drift 1879, "Pinned Like Rats in a Hole"*; Osprey Campaign Series #41, Osprey Publishing 1996, ISBN 1-85532-506-3

Battle of Isandlwana – 1879
Coupland, Sir Reginald (1948) *Zulu Battle Piece: Isandhlwana,* London.

Gunfight at the O.K. Corral – 1881
Grace McCool (1990). *Gunsmoke: The True Story of Old Tombstone.* Tucson: Treasure Chest Publications, Inc. ISBN 0-918080-52-5.

Battle of San Juan Hill – 1898
Roosevelt, Theodore, *The Rough Riders,* Scribner's Magazine, Vol. 25, January–June 1899, New York: Charles Scribner's Sons,

Battle of Saragarhi – 1897
Jay Singh- Sohal (2013) *Saragarhi: The Forgotten Battle,* Birmingham: Dot Hyphen Publishers, (ISBN 978-0957054073)

Battle of Tannenberg, WWI – 1914
Tuchman, Barbara Wertheim (1994), *The Guns of August,* New York: Ballantine Books, ISBN 978-0-345-47609-8

Battle of Nek, WWI – 1915
Roadbent, Harvey (2005) *Gallipoli: The Fatal Shore.* Camberwell, Victoria: Viking/Penguin Press. ISBN 978-0-670-04085-8

Burness, Peter (1996). The Nek: The Tragic Charge of the Light Horse at Gallipoli. *ISBN 0-86417-782-8*

Battle Kut El Amara, WWI – 1916
Gardner, Nikolas (2004). "Sepoys and the Siege of Kut-al-Amara, December 1915 –April 1961". *War in History.*

Battle of Verdun, WWI – 1916
Evans, M. M. (2004). Battles of World War I. Devizes: Select Editions. ISBN 1-84193-226-4.

Battle of Eben Emael, WWII – 1940
Frieser, Karl-Heinz; Greenwood, John T. (2005), The Blitzkrieg Legend: The 1940 Campaign in the West, Annapolis: Naval Institute Press, ISBN 978-1-59114-294-2

Battle of Stalingrad, WWII – 1942–1943
Clark, Alan. (1965). Barbarossa: the Russian-German Conflict, 1941–45. OCLC 154155228

Bellamy, Chris (2007). Absolute War: Soviet Russia in the Second World War. New York: Alfred A. Knopf & Random House. ISBN 978-0-375-41086-4.

Battle of the Bulge, WWII – DEC 1944–JAN 1945
Ambrose, Stephen. (1992), Band of Brothers, New York: Simon & Schuster, ISBN 0-671-76922-7

Liddell Hart, Basil Henry (1970), History of the Second World War, G. P. Putnam's Sons., ISBN 978-0-306-80912-5

Battle at the Chosin Reservoir-Korean War – 1950
Halberstam, David. (2007), The Coldest Winter – America and the Korean War, New York, New York: Hyperion, ISBN 978-1-4013-0052-4

Bay of Pigs Invasion, Cuba – 1961
Bohning, Don. (2005). *The Castro Obsession: U.S. Covert Operations Against Cuba, 1959–1965.* Washington, D.C.: Potomac Books, Inc. *ISBN 978-1-57488-676-4.*

Desert Shield & Desert Storm – Gulf War Iraq 1991 and Operation Iraqi Freedom 2003–2011

Hiro, Dilip. (1992). *Desert Shield to Desert Storm: The Second Gulf War.* Routledge. *ISBN 978-0-415-90657-9.*

Finlan, Alastair (2003). *The Gulf War 1991.* Osprey. *ISBN 978-1-84176-574-7.*

Spencer C. Tucker. *(2015–12–14). U.S. Conflicts in the 21st Century: Afghanistan War, Iraq War, and the War on Terror. ISBN 978-1440838798*

COPYRIGHTS

Location	Credit	Source
Page 3	Okanakdeniz	© Okanakdeniz | Dreamstime.com
Page 8	Ernest Meissonier	Musee d'Orsay
Page 9	Carl Wahlbom	National Museum of Stockholm
Page 10	Illustrator Unknown	Cornwall Historical Society
Page 11	Senatorjoanna	© Senatorjoanna | Dreamstime.com
Page 12	Kaido Rummel	© Kaido Rummel | Dreamstime.com
Page 13	Anthony Baggett	© Anthony Baggett | Dreamstime.com
Page 15	Francois Pascal Simon Gerard	www.napoleon-empire.com
Page 17	Fortunino Matania	Crisis Magazine, www.crisismagazine.com, 10 APRIL 2015 A New History of the Crusades Obama Should Read, by Stephanie Pacheco
Page 19	Ratpack2	© Ratpack2 | Dreamstime.com
Page 22	Guantana	© Guantana | Dreamstime.com
Page 23	US Army Photo	NPR. History Dept
Page 24	Elena Plekhanova	© Elena Plekhanova | Dreamstime.com
Page 25	Joseph Golby	© Joseph Golby | Dreamstime.com

Page 27	Paul Topp	© Paul Topp | Dreamstime.com
Page 28	Vasily Maksimov	www.ancient-origins.net/history/golden-horde
Page 29	Artist Unknown	U.S. Navy Courtesy of chinfo.navy.mil
Page 31	Michal Stipek	© Michal Stipek | Dreamstime.com
Page 32	Tupungato	© Tupungato | Dreamstime.com
Page 34	Oknebulog	© Oknebulog | Dreamstime.com
Page 35	Photographer Unkown	6 Modern Technologies Animals Invented Millions of Years Ago. Cracked.com & 7 Weird Weapons of WWII, realitypod.com
Page 36	Chorazin3d	© Chorazin3d | Dreamstime.com
Page 37	Phtographer Unkown	Rock Island Auction
Page 38	Anton Starikov	© Anton Starikov | Dreamstime.com
Page 39	Photographer Unkown	ebay.ie, etsy.com, sableimages.com, antiqueauctionsnow.net
Page 40	Mark Eaton	© Mark Eaton | Dreamstime.com
Page 41	Ming Xu	© Ming Xu | Dreamstime.com
Page 43	Photographer Unkown	The Ridiculously Oversized Punt Gun, www.todayfoundout.com, The Punt Gun: Enemy to Waterfowl, www.historybyztim.com, www.reddit.com, www.pinterest.com
Page 44	Rashīd al-Dīn's History of the World, 1307	Edinburgh University Library, Scotland, Hungary History, ww.brittanica.com, or Techniques & Triumphs of the Military Horesman, Edited by James Lawford, Crescent Books, 1982

Page 45	Ruslan Gilmanshin	© Ruslan Gilmanshin	Dreamstime.com
Page 47	Edgar S. Paxon	The Definitive Visual History of War from Bronze Age Battles to 21st Century Conflict, Saul David Editor, Dorling Kindersley Limited Publishers, 2009 & also Buffalo Bill Center of the West< whitney Westr Art Museum, Montana
Page 49	Mario Savoia	© Mario Savoia	Dreamstime.com
Page 50	John Steeple Davis	en.Wikipedia.org
Page 52	Photographer Unkown	Mapio.net -Facebook
Page 53	Konstantinos Papaloannou	© Konstantinos Papaioannou	Dreamstime.com
Page 53	Amitaj	© Amitai	Dreamstime.com
Page 55	Alfonsodetemos	© Alfonsodetomas	Dreamstime.com
Page 57	Daniel Eskridge	© Daniel Eskridge	Dreamstime.com
Page 59	Oleg Nesterkin	© Oleg Nesterkin	Dreamstime.com
Page 60	Meoita	© Meoita	Dreamstime.com
Page 62	Ryan Beiler	© Rrodrickbeiler	Dreamstime.com
Page 63	Jaroslaw Grudzinski	© Jaroslaw Grudzinski	Dreamstime.com
Page 64	Kevin George	© Kevin George	Dreamstime.com
Page 66	Bonnie Avonrude	© Bonnie Avonrude	Dreamstime.com
Page 69	Thomas Dutour	© Thomas Dutour	Dreamstime.com

Page 69	Vladiczech	© Vladiczech | Dreamstime.com
Page 70	Artist Unknown	Jean Danjou -Wikimedia Commons
Page 72	American Spirit	© Joe Sohm | Dreamstime.com
Page 73	Niwit Meedej	© Niwit Meedej | Dreamstime.com
Page 75	U.S. Army	U.S. Army Regimental Coin
Page 76	Jeremy Richards	© Jeremy Richards | Dreamstime.com
Page 78	Steff22	© Stef22 | Dreamstime.com
Page 79	Lemuel Francis Abbott	Horatio Nelson at www.royalnavy.mod.uk or National Portrait Gallery, London England
Page 80	Anthony Baggett	© Anthony Baggett | Dreamstime.com
Page 82	Richard Caton Woodville	National Army Musuem, London, England at collection.nam.ac.uk online collection or Commons.Wikimedia.org & History.com
Page 83	Photographer Unkown	Gettysburgdaily.com, Jim Hessler, Sickles at Gettysburg 10 JUNE 2009
Page 85	Jess Ignacio Murguizu Bacaicoa	© Jesus Ignacio Murguizu Bacaicoa | Dreamstime.com
Page 87	Tarik Gok	© Tarik Gok | Dreamstime.com
Page 90	Sadik Gulec	© Sadık Güleç | Dreamstime.com
Page 91	Adam Jones	Nek Cemetery, 18MAY2011 posted on Flickr on 21JUNE2011 by Labattlblueboy or Commons.Wikimedia.org
Page 93	Donna Kilday	© Donna Kilday | Dreamstime.com

Page 94	May 15, 1718 patent	Daily Courant March 1722
Page 95	Photographer Unkown	Tsar tank on Tumblr -www.tumbler.com, About World War I, 1914 Worlds First Heavy Bomber is Russion, hubpages.com or Strange Tanks, historum.com
Page 97	Photographer Unkown	The 5 Worst Modern Production Firearms The Truth About Guns, Range 365, www.thetruthaboutguns.com or 9gag.com or militaryarms.ru
Page 99	Illustrator Unknown	Commons.Wikipedia.org, forum.worldwarships.com, Round Ships of the Russian Admiral at englishrussia.com & World of Warships
Page 101	Photographer Unkown	Strange Weapons of WWII at www.unfinishedman.com, Top Five Bizarre Weapons of WW II at www.youtube.com, scout.com or listverse.com
Page 102	Photographer Unkown	German Wind Cannon at www.ww2f.com, disaircraftgreyfalcon.us or 15 Most Fearsome German Wonder Weapons of WWII at www.chaostrophic.com
Page 103		Project Habbakuk Britian's Secret Ice "Bergship"Aircraft Carrier Project at 99percentvisible.org or History with Phil, The Ice Ship Cometh a mfame.guru or www.gonder.org or The Colossus that Never Was at osnetdaily.com
Page 105	Photographer Unkown	Strange & Weird Airplanes of the World att realitypod.com or Soviet Giant K-7 Bomber at tieba.baidu.com

Page 106	Photographer Unkown	World War II in Pictures: Tiger Tanks - dated 23SEP2013 at world-wartow.filminspector.com, Germany needs an amphibious tank too- 23SEP 2013 at www.reddit.com
Page 108	Photographer Unkown	The 6 most Ill-Conceived Weapons ever Built-10JUNE2011 at www.cracked.com or The 2 worst weapons of WWII were masterpieces from the Commonwealth 19JAN2018 at mil-new.sina.com.cn/history/2018
Page 109	Photographer Unkown	uncylopedia.wikia.com or 1956 Vintage Photos: armoured Vespa Scooter with Cannon posted 18 JUNE 2013 at www.freerepublic.com
Page 110	Illustrator Unknown	en.Wikipedia.org or The 10 worst US Aircraft 1JUNE2016 at hushkit.net or XF-85 Goblin War Thunder at forum.warthunder.com
Page 112	U.S. Navy Photo 18 MARCH 2003	War Animals at oneclickwonders.wordpress.com or Navy Dolphin Patrol Under Fire 28JAN2009 at www.wired.com
Page 113	US Airforce via AP	National Public Radio – NPR.org
Page 115	U.S. Army Photo	ARDEC Engineers Develop Solid State Active Denial Technology for Non Lethal Crowd control 12OCT2016 at www.army.mil
Page 115	U.S. Army Photo	How Today's military is using lasers to blow thing up and light stuff on fire, 22JULY2011 by Ed Grabianowski at io9.gizmodo.com

Page 116	Serhii Selin	© Serhii Selin | Dreamstime.com
Page 117	Photo Taken 8/8/2014	© Dezzor | Dreamstime.com
Page 119		Part 2 When The Gun Explodes in Your Hands 6SEP2015 at youlove-gunsandzombies.blogspot.com
Page 119	U.S. Army Photo	U.S Army Operator's Manual for M16, M16A1 Rifle and Field Manual FM 3-22.9 Rifle Marsksman Ship M16A1, M16A2/3, M16A4 & M4 Carbine April 2003
Page 120	Photographer Unkown	Battle of Fort Sumter & Confederate Army of the Potomac at en.Wikipedia.org or Civil War Photos and Images at www.civil-war.net
Page 121	Pablo Utrilla	© Pablo Utrilla | Dreamstime.com
Page 124	Everett Collection Inc.	© Everett Collection Inc. | Dreamstime.com
Page 125	Mesut Do?an	© Mesut Doğan | Dreamstime.com
Page 127	Photographer Unkown	Fight-squad.com
Page 129	Alexandr Bilnov	© Alexandr Blinov | Dreamstime.com
Page 131	Kolotype	© Kolotype | Dreamstime.com
Page 131	Sergey Khakimullin	© Sergey Khakimullin | Dreamstime.com
Page 132	Mr 1805	© Mr1805 | Dreamstime.com
Page 133	Kurz & Allison	U.S. Library of Congress & Stonewall Jackson Injured by Friendly Fire at www.historytoday.com

Page 135	Robert Zehetmayer	© Robert Zehetmayer | Dreamstime.com
Page 135	Bob Suir	© Bob Suir | Dreamstime.com
Page 137	Geronimo36	© Geronimo36 | Dreamstime.com
Page 139	Photographer Unkown	National Museum of Australia at www.nma.gov.au
Page 140	Photographer Unkown	1922: Robert Erskin Childers, for carrying a gun of Michael Collins - Article dated 24NOV2008 at www.executedtoday.com
Page 142	Photographer Unkown	Epic Land Battles, Richard Holmes, Edited by S.L. Mayer Peerage Books 1976
Page 143	Eugenesergeev	© Eugenesergeev | Dreamstime.com
Page 145	Jerome Correia	© Jeromecorreia | Dreamstime.com
Page 148	Artist Unknown	Siege of Alesia Ends: Rebellious Gauls Defeated, Julius Caesar Triumphs, 5OCT2011 at www.burnpit.us or en.Wikipedia.org
Page 150	Lionel Noel Royer	The Roman Army. The Greatest War Machine of the Ancient world. Editor ChrisMcNab, Metro Books, New York, 2013 & Siege of Alesia Ends: Rebellious Gauls Defeated, Julius Caesar Triumphs, 5OCT2011 at www.burnpit.us or en.Wikipedia.org
Page 151	Elena Duvernay	© Elena Duvernay | Dreamstime.com
Page 153	Gunold	© Gunold | Dreamstime.com
Page 155	Jean Adrien Guignet	The Louvre Museum in Paris, France

Page 156	Phil Cold	© Philcold | Dreamstime.com	
Page 157	Artist Unknown	Mary Evans Picture Library, London, England & These Generals Were the Closest of Enemies by Peggy Noonan 24MAY2018 at www.wsj.com	
Page 158	Photographer Unkown	German Tiger Tanks, Part 2 at www.worldwarphotos.info/gallery/Germany/tanks-2-3/tiger	
Page 159	Artist Unknown	Did Germany Lose WWII because of a lack of oil rather than the wrong war strategis at www.quoro.com or Strategy for Defeat: The Luftwaffe 1933-1945 by Williamson Murray at www.ibiblio.org	
Page 161	Photographer Unkown	Battle of the Bulge Then and Now, Jean Paul Pallud, Battle of Britain Prints International Limited, 1984	
Page 162	Douglas Wojtarowicz	© Douglas Wojtarowicz | Dreamstime.com	
Page 164	Mulikov	© Mulikov | Dreamstime.com	
Page 164	Creative-commons-tockphotos	Creativecommonstockphotos | Dreamstime.com	
Page 165	Shane photographs	© Shanephotographs | Dreamstime.com	
Page 167	Artist Unknown	National Army Museum, Chelsea, London, NAM Accession # NAM.1960-09-35-2 -The Siege of Kut Al Amara: World War 1 at www.learning-history.com	
Page 168	Ktarrier	© Ktarrier | Dreamstime.com	

Page 168	Steve Estvanik	© Steve Estvanik | Dreamstime.com
Page 169	Ishaccm	© Ishaccm | Dreamstime.com
Page 171	Photographer Unkown	Military Intelligence-Fail at www.flickr.com or Photo Gallery for Korean Daily at blog.koreadaily.com
Page 172	Alphonse de Neuville	Art Gallery of New South Wales, Sydney, Australia & en.Wikipedia.org
Page 173	André Castaigne	Scythed Chariot at en.Wikipedia.org or The Charge of the Persian Scythed Chariots at Guaugamela at commons.wikimedia.org
Page 175	Otto Albert Koch	10 Major Roman Military Defeats at www.toptenz.net
Page 177	Ekaterina Bykova	© Ekaterina Bykova | Dreamstime.com
Page 178	Vadim Demianovich	© Vadim Demianovich | Dreamstime.com
Page 178	Photographer Unkown	World War II, Ronald Heiferman, Edited by S.L. Mayer, Peerage Books, 1973
Page 180	Wilhelm Camphausen	Prince Otto Von Bismark at www.newegg.com or www.allposters.com
Page 182	Photographer Unkown	atlantic.com 27APR2014 World War I in Photos: Global Conflict
Page 183	Stanley Berkeley	Stanley Berkeley at commons.Wikipedia.org
Page 184	Robert Alexander Hillingford	Warfare History Network, Waterloo, 24SEP2018 at warefarehistorynetwork.com or Battle of Waterloo at www.history.com/topics/british-history/battle-of-waterloo or Napaleon'd Defeat at the Battle of Waterloo, www.historywiz.com or Robert Alexander Hillingford at en.Wikipedia.org

Page 185	Milkovasa	© Milkovasa | Dreamstime.com
Page 186	Patrick Breig	© Patrick Breig | Dreamstime.com
Page 187	Artist Unknown	Anglo-Japanese Alliance at en.Wikipedia.org
Page 188	William Rossin	© William Rossin | Dreamstime.com
Page 189	Baron Francois Pascal Simon Gerard	Battle of Austerlitz at www.napoleon-empire.com
Page 191	Renaud Philippe	© Renaud Philippe | Dreamstime.com
Page 193	Bogdan Willewalde	Retreat Scene from Russian-French War 1812 at napoleon1812.wordpress.com
Page 194	Photographer Unknown	National Archives, Washington, D.C.
Page 195	Dragan Ilic'	© Dragan Ilic | Dreamstime.com
Page 196	Ktarrier	© Ktarrier | Dreamstime.com
Page 197	Dalius Baranauskas	© Dalius Baranauskas | Dreamstime.com
Page 198	Oleg Zabielin	© Oleg Zabielin | Dreamstime.com
Page 199	Oleg Zabielin	© Oleg Zabielin | Dreamstime.com
Page 199	Oleg Zabielin	© Oleg Zabielin | Dreamstime.com
Page 200	Algol	© Algol | Dreamstime.com
Page 200	American Spirit	© Joe Sohm | Dreamstime.com
Page 201	Scaramax	© Scaramax | Dreamstime.com
Page 203	Oleg Zabielin	© Oleg Zabielin | Dreamstime.com
Page 204	Jasmina	© Jasmina | Dreamstime.com
Page 205	Photographer Unkown	Vietnam War Body Count Controversy at en.Wikipedia.org

Page 208	Royalty Free Stock Photos	© Matthieuclouis | Dreamstime.com
Page 208	Artist Unknown	Military History Now.com
Page 210	Artist Unknown	Trebuchet at En.Wikipedia.org or The Life of Genghis Kan timeline at www.timetoast.com
Page 212	Everett Collection Inc.	© Everett Collection Inc. | Dreamstime.com
Page 214	Chabkc	© Chabkc | Dreamstime.com
Page 214	Photographer Unkown	Ordnance QF 18-pounder or Artillery of World War I at en.Wikipedia.org
Page 216	Mikael Damkier	© Mikael Damkier | Dreamstime.com
Page 219	Konstaantin Markov	© Konstantin Markov | Dreamstime.com
Page 220	Tomas Popelka	© Tomas Popelka | Dreamstime.com
Page 201	Photographer-london	© Photographerlondon | Dreamstime.com
Page 222	Photographer Unknown	
Page 223	Artist Unknown	U.S. Army Training Manual FM 23-2, Light Armor Weapons

Rate this book on our website!

www.novumpublishing.com

The author

Jeff Carr served in both command and staff assignments in the US Army Infantry and Special Operations units (Airborne). He also served as a Battalion Operations Officer (S-3) for a Foreign Internal Defense and Unconventional Warfare Unit in Mosul, Iraq from 2004–2005 and as a Tactics instructor at the US Army Command and General Staff College. He is a light weapons expert and military history buff.

novum 🔖 PUBLISHER FOR NEW AUTHORS

The publisher

> *He who stops getting better stops being good.*

This is the motto of novum publishing, and our focus is on finding new manuscripts, publishing them and offering long-term support to the authors.
Our publishing house was founded in 1997, and since then it has become THE expert for new authors and has won numerous awards.

Our editorial team will peruse each manuscript within a few weeks free of charge and without obligation.

You will find more information about
novum publishing and our books on the internet:

w w w . n o v u m p u b l i s h i n g . c o m

www.ingramcontent.com/pod-product-compliance
Lightning Source LLC
Chambersburg PA
CBHW060836170426
43192CB00019BA/2792